NATIONAL GEOGRAPHIC DIRECTIONS

ALSO BY GARRY WILLS

Mr. Jefferson's University

GARRY WILLS

Mr. Jefferson's University

NATIONAL GEOGRAPHIC DIRECTIONS

NATIONAL GEOGRAPHIC
Washington, D.C.

Published by the National Geographic Society
1145 17th Street, N.W., Washington, D.C. 20036-4688

Text copyright © 2002 Garry Wills

First printing November 2002
Paperback edition 2006, ISBN-10: 0-7922-5560-7, ISBN-13: 978-0-7922-5560-4

Library of Congress Cataloging-in-Publication Data
Wills, Garry, 1934 -
    Mr. Jefferson's university / Garry Wills.
      p. cm. – (National Geographic directions)
    ISBN 0-7922-6531-9 (hard)
    1. University of Virginia–Buildings–History–19th Century. 2. Jefferson, Thomas
1743-1826–Contributions in architecture. I. Title: Mister Jefferson's university. II. Title.
III. Series

LD5678.3 .W55 2002
378.755'481–dc21

                                                        2002035258

One of the world's largest nonprofit scientific and educational organizations, the National Geographic Society was founded in 1888 "for the increase and diffusion of geographic knowledge." Fulfilling this mission, the Society educates and inspires millions every day through its magazines, books, television programs, videos, maps and atlases, research grants, the National Geographic Bee, teacher workshops, and innovative classroom materials. The Society is supported through membership dues, charitable gifts, and income from the sale of its educational products. This support is vital to National Geographic's mission to increase global understanding and promote conservation of our planet through exploration, research, and education.
For more information, please call 1-800-NGS LINE (647-5463), write to the Society at the above address, or visit the Society's Web site at www.nationalgeographic.com.

Printed in the U.S.A.

To Garry L.

"I'll put a girdle round about the earth."

CONTENTS

Mr. Jefferson's University

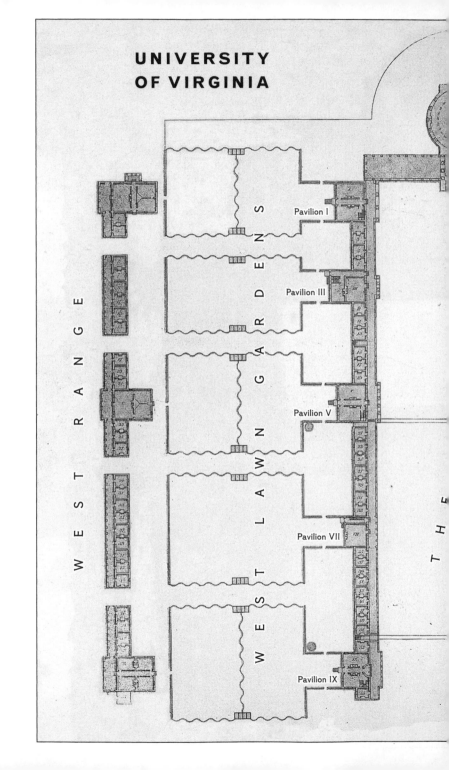

UNIVERSITY OF VIRGINIA

WEST RANGE

GARDENS

WEST LAWN

Pavilion I

Pavilion III

Pavilion V

Pavilion VII

Pavilion IX

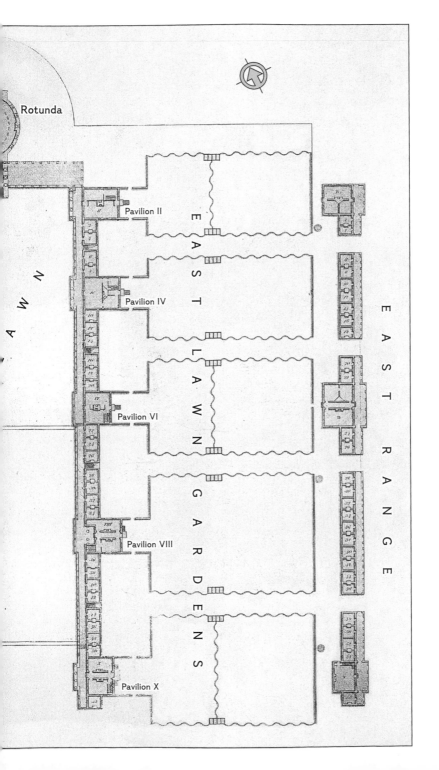

Rotunda

Pavilion II

Pavilion IV

Pavilion VI

Pavilion VIII

Pavilion X

E A S T   L A W N   G A R D E N S

E A S T   R A N G E

L A W N

Key to Brief Citations

A date given alone refers to an entry of that day in the Library of Congress Correspondence of Thomas Jefferson, available online from the Library.

A date preceded by the letter C refers to a Joseph Cabell letter of that day in *Early History of the University of Virginia as Contained in the Letters of Thomas Jefferson and Joseph C. Cabell* (J. W. Randolph, 1856).

Numbers preceded by the letter G refer to chapter and page in Frank Edgar Grizzard, Jr., "Documentary History of the Construction of the Buildings at the University of Virginia, 1817-1828," Doctoral Dissertation, University of Virginia, 1996, available online from the library of the University of Virginia.

Preface

Asked by National Geographic to write about a favorite place I visit often, I rejected Venice, since I had already written a book about it. I turned my gaze back to America. When I began writing a book about Jefferson in the early 1970s, I made several tours of the remaining Virginia plantations, to see the world that produced him. The principal plantation, of course, the one I went to see most often, was Jefferson's own, Monticello. But I found the university at the foot of his mountain in some ways even more complex, complete, and endlessly fascinating than the home perched above it. Over the years, as I have gone back there year by year, the university has become more convincingly a reflection of Jefferson's entire personality, its naive flaws as well as its towering strengths. I came, at last, to realize that its construction was accomplished only by a series of truly heroic acts.

GARRY WILLS
September 2002

PROLOGUE

Jefferson as Artist

> {I} *Prospero the prime duke, being so reputed*
> *In dignity, and for the liberal arts*
> *Without a parallel, those being all my study ...*
> —THE TEMPEST 1.2.73-74

Jefferson is the only president of the United States who was also a great artist. Other presidents have noodled at the keyboard or daubed at easels. But Jefferson was a building architect of large ambition and achievement, as well as a landscape architect and an interior designer. There are no exact parallels, at least in Western culture, for this combination of political and aesthetic prominence. There are stray examples of major political figures who were artistically creative—Charles d'Orléans, perhaps, for his Renaissance poetry, or Jan Paderewski for his music (which he composed as well as performed), or Václav Havel for his plays. But Charles was royal by birth, and spent most of his life rhyming away in prison. Paderewski and Havel were mainly artists who ended their careers as leaders of, respectively, Poland and the Czech Republic. Benjamin Disraeli's career similarly falls into two parts, the first as novelist, the second as prime minister.

Jefferson, by contrast, worked all his life at statecraft *and* at visionary building. He was commissioned to draw plans for extending William and Mary's Wren Building three years before he composed his first political document; and he ended his long life just as he completed the seventeen buildings of the University of Virginia's original plan. To combine the prose of power and the poetry of art, at a high and continuing level, is something no one else did. In *The Tempest,* Shakespeare made Prospero neglect government while perfecting his art:

> And to my state grew stranger, being transported
> And rapt in secret studies. (1.2.76-77)

At the end of the play, Prospero renounces his art to resume his political status. But Jefferson, unlike Prospero, managed to work simultaneously on his political and his artistic tasks. In the time between his first amateur effort and the masterful completion of his university, Jefferson designed beautiful homes for himself and others; gave Virginia's State Capitol the first Roman temple form on American soil; and worked closely with Benjamin Latrobe on the creation of the federal city. He is this country's most influential architect, since he established an ethos and a rationale for our public buildings. His great author-ity bound us, for good or ill, to a sense that ancient Roman forms express civic responsibility and gravitas.

His greatest artwork was the cluster of buildings in Charlottesville that he called his "academical village." There he launched and completed what was the largest construction project since the development of the federal city itself—in whose construction he had also played a part. In 1976, when the American Institute of Architects polled professional critics and practitioners for "the proudest achievement in American architecture," Jefferson's University came in first (Rockefeller Center was second, Saarinen's Dulles Airport and Wright's Fallingwater tied for third). In 2001, the World Heritage Convention identified only eighteen world treasures in the United States, and the university was joined with Monticello as one of those eighteen. There was no other domestic building listed along with Monticello, and only one other public building (Independence Hall in Philadelphia) was listed along with the university.

Jefferson's artistry was not a mere indulgence, a form of dilettantism. He worked from a profound aesthetic of art's moral, political, and pedagogical importance. He was, moreover, a man whose creativity deepened and became bolder with age. Some men or women have a creative breakthrough, followed by a period of development (prolonged or curtailed, as the case may be), fading at last into pale repetition or faltering energy. But certain creators—a Beethoven, a Titian—go from strength to strength up to the moment of their death. Verdi created his two greatest operas when he was seventy-four *(Otello)* and eighty *(Falstaff)*. Jefferson's retirement from the presidency in his sixties led to stunning new work at Monticello and his second home (Poplar Forest), culminating in the nine years of the university's creation. His grasp grew firmer, his vision clearer, with age. Working at a strenuous pace from 1817 to 1826, he passed from his seventy-fourth to his eighty-third year in this final creative act. As his own body's

FIGURE I. *The Lawn in 1909*

fabric was disintegrating, he poured his spirit into a physical
expression of intellectual activity. In the shapes of the buildings, interconnected but highly individual, a little cosmos of
learning took shape, a musical dance of forms, a microcosm of
his beloved Newtonian scheme of things.

The university's patterns have largely been retained to this
day, and their intended effect can still be experienced. The
whole complex has an intricate unity—one that Jefferson
expounded to Lafayette when he showed him around and
through it during the French hero's visit to America in 1825.
The overall pattern is made clear in an engraving Jefferson had
made by Peter Maverick in 1822, to advertise his project to the
state Assembly, future professors, and potential students
(FRONTISPIECE). There are four rows of buildings. The inner
two rows are made up of ten Pavilions (professors' homes and
classrooms), five on either side of a central Lawn, leading up to

the high Rotunda that holds the library (FIGURE 1). The two outer rows (Ranges) are made up of six "Hotels" (service buildings), three on each side. The buildings on all four rows are connected by a row of small student rooms (Jefferson called them dormitories), with a continuous colonnade before them on the Lawn, and a continuous arcade before them on the Ranges (FIGURE 2). The rows of dormitories/colonnades/arcades are the ligaments that tie the whole together organically.

The Maverick engraving can be deceptive. It gives a greater sense of overriding order than one actually experiences as one moves through this complex. The Lawn is the top of a ridge from which, on either side, the ground falls off irregularly. The topography makes buildings play hide and seek with each other. From either Range one goes up toward the Lawn past gardens enclosed in wavy (serpentine) walls (FIGURE 3). From these sloping gardens one catches glimpses of the high Rotunda's dome, or of the three-story backs of the Pavilions

FIGURE 2. *The West Range*

(which seem to have only two stories on the Lawn itself). No matter how one comes at it, this interplay of structures combines the expectable with the surprising. It can seem, moment by moment, transparently linear or densely labyrinthine. The large lines of the plan are fitted to the resistant and enriching site. It only becomes clear with repeated exposure how deftly Jefferson has used a great ridge—grading its top to open up the central Lawn in three terraces, then using the flanks that fall off from it for supporting and complicating elements. The tailoring of the different elements to the anfractuous ground brings out all of Jefferson's artistry—much as Michelangelo triumphed over the bungled stone he was given for carving his "David."

The first way to approach the university, the one Jefferson intended, is from the south end of the sloping central Lawn.

FIGURE 3. *View toward the Lawn*

From there one ascends the three terraces, moving between the facing Pavilions toward the Rotunda at the north end (FIGURE 1). Today one must maneuver around three buildings, added later to close off the south end of the Lawn, in order to begin this ascent. As you look toward the Rotunda from the original entry point, its huge Corinthian columns seem to stand on the ground. Only as you go up the Lawn does a high tribune on which the Rotunda stands come into view, along with the bases of the higher Pavilions' columns.

The Pavilion facades vary in size and character, punctuating the row of little Tuscan columns that runs between and through (or around) their classical elevations. Some Pavilions advance colossal columns, beyond this Tuscan colonnade, out onto the Lawn. Some draw back from the line, in tactful

Figure 4. *Pavilion VII*

Figure 5. *Pavilion VIII*

counterpoint to the more forward buildings. The Tuscan colonnade must check and resume its rhythms to accommodate these variations. The columns negotiate the changing levels of the terrace, sometimes with a slight turning of the row, using doubled columns to effect the transition—dotted notes to break up the monotony. Engagement with or negotiation around the Pavilions calls for constant little deferences. In one case, the Tuscan colonnade is actually suspended, the gap in it filled in by an arcade that is part of Pavilion VII (FIGURE 4). The rhythm of the colonnade is thus being constantly varied, here checked, there urged forward, sometimes missing a beat, sometimes doubling it. The elements in this scheme are engaged in omnidirectional diplomacy with each other. At Pavilion VIII, for instance, the columns shorten their intervals near the Pavilion, and turn a right angle, using two close-set columns to step out onto the Lawn and hold the projecting deck above them (FIGURE 5). At Pavilion V, two Tuscan columns are set close together to start the run on a lower terrace (FIGURE 6).

The connecting student rooms seem lined up with monotonous regularity, though in fact the number of rooms between Pavilions is rarely the same on the east Lawn and the west Lawn. The differing numbers are determined by the varying widths of the Pavilion facades to be connected, and by varyingly spaced exit passages leading down to the gardens on either side. The different styles of the Pavilion facades lead to their not being centered on each others' axis—an effect apparent in the first two Pavilions by the Rotunda—the central door of Pavilion I is farther south than that of Pavilion II which faces it, and the same is true of the facing Pavilions IX and X.

FIGURE 6. *Pavilion V*

In another manifestation of variety, the space between Pavilions is progressively increased as one moves away from the Rotunda. This plays different tricks on the eye according to whether one looks from the north or the south. From the south, the longer space between the nearest Pavilions is presumed to continue throughout the series, making the Rotunda seem farther off than it is. But if one looks from the other direction, the longer spaces at the end compensate for foreshortening, making the spaces look regular precisely because they are not. This subtle effect is increased by the fact that the terrace levels are also lengthened as they recede from the Rotunda, with a corollary widening of the gardens along the flanks—these details can be seen on the Maverick engraving (FRONTISPIECE).

Despite the overall impression of order, we are forewarned as we approach the south end of the Lawn that the two ranks of

FIGURE 7. *Pavilion IX*

Pavilions will offer diversity, since the last two Pavilions, those closest to us, are markedly different in size and style—Pavilion IX on our left (FIGURE 7) seems low and modern, with its engaged columns partially hidden by the colonnade, while Pavilion X on our right (FIGURE 8) is tall and formal, with the only colossal order on this half of the Lawn (FIGURE 1). The intentional contrast is clearly marked in an early drawing of the Rotunda with these terminal Pavilions in the foreground (FIGURE 17, p.100). The use of these Pavilions as both continuous with the general scheme and yet terminating it is marked in several ways. They are set off from the others by a drop in the terrace, and by the fact that, on this lower level, where they stand alone on each side of the Lawn, they have only one student room (not a row of them) on either side of it. These rooms thus look like balancing wings to each Pavilion, putting a full stop to the

FIGURE 8. *Pavilion X*

series. They are also set apart from the rest of the colonnade by a clustering of columns before these last student rooms. The rooms are interpretable in two ways, as continuous with the colonnade or as special adjuncts to the terminal Pavilions. Jefferson composes with finesse, subtlety, and deliberate ambiguity.

Jefferson achieved what Ruskin called "a daring variation of pretended symmetry," escaping "the lower or vulgar unity of rigid law."

> There is sensation in every inch of it, and an accommodation to every architectural necessity, with a determined variation in arrangement, which is exactly like the related proportions and provisions in the structure of organic form.[1]

The overall effect is paradoxical—of regimentation and individual expression, of hierarchical order *and* relaxed improvising. Some seize on only one aspect of this complicated experience, calling it either too orderly and systematic or too heterogeneous and disordered. But it is the reconciliation of these apparent irreconcilables that is the genius of the system. The plan expresses the conflicting values of the education Jefferson envisaged, which was a mix of the prescriptive and the self-determining, of the fixed and the free. Authoritative teaching was offered to students, who were nonetheless left to fashion their own course through the school, since Jefferson provided for an entirely elective curriculum.

Jefferson has, in some areas, come under criticism in recent years, diminishing the almost automatic reverence he once commanded. But his art has been earning greater acceptance and understanding, reflected in the high degree of professionalism now directed to the study, interpretation, and preservation of his major artifacts. And the peak of that art is the "academical village" in Charlottesville, which has never ceased to perform its teaching function in the 177 years since it opened its doors to students. The university represented a disciplined freedom. Its very shapes said that the pursuit of truth is a joyful burden. Students began their pursuit of learning by learning the meaning of the structures they inhabited.

CHAPTER ONE

The Struggle to Create

On October 6, 1817, about a mile from the tiny village of Charlottesville, Virginia, there was an odd thronging of people through an open field. It would not take an acute observer long to see what the occasion was. Freemasons were there, in full regalia, in a procession of the sort reserved for laying important cornerstones. On they came, in graded ranks—tile-layers with swords drawn, apprentices, fellows, masters, past masters, stewards, deacons, secretaries, treasurers, wardens, visiting masters, substitutes, and the grand master and chaplain. (G 1.14) Following them were bearers of the corn and oil and wine used in the Masonic ceremonies, and a designated orator (Valentine Southall), and a marching band. This might seem a disproportionately grand way to begin constructing one building for a regional academy (Central College), one no different from other local schools in Virginia, Hampden-Sidney say, or

Washington College (it would later be Washington and Lee). The humpbacked site was cut and scarred with ongoing efforts to grade it, placing the new building asymmetrically on the western edge of a ridge of land more carefully leveled. Piles of freshly kilned bricks stood ready for use. White workers and black slaves moved around the outskirts of the crowd, waiting for it to disperse so they could go to work on the construction.

The reason such a large crowd had assembled became clear when the Masonic grand master handed "the implements used by our ancient fraternity"—the square, the plumb, and the level—to the man who would formally lay the cornerstone. This man was the President of the United States, James Monroe, who had come from Washington just for this event. He was a member of the six-man board of Central College, as were two former presidents who attended the ceremony—Thomas Jefferson and James Madison. The three had marched abreast in the procession, followed by a second rank of their fellow board members. William Thornton, the architect of the United States Capitol, when he read a newspaper report of the event, wrote to Jefferson: "I was also pleased to see an account of the meeting of such distinguished characters as the three presidents of the United States on so praiseworthy an occasion. How different to the meeting of the three emperors on the continent of Europe, after a bloody battle!" (G 1.6-7)

Jefferson, who was the elected rector of the college's board, had filled that body with names important at both the local and national level. This show of respectability seemed out of proportion to the modesty of the institution they were to steer. But Jefferson did not mean for it to remain modest. He had already inflated it once, and was poised to do so again, immediately after this ceremony. His first step had been to take direction, in 1814, of a phantom school, Albemarle Academy, which had been given a state charter in 1804 but had raised no buildings. Within two years he had persuaded the General Assembly of Virginia to upgrade the phantom academy into a projected Central College. The name was carefully chosen, making the point that its Albemarle site was less peripheral to the state than the College of William and Mary to the east or than fledgling or projected academies to the west (Washington College, Hampden-Sidney, and a planned college at Staunton). As soon as the cornerstone was laid, Jefferson meant to plead for a second upgrading, this time to university status. If he could get funding from the state, this first building would soon be joined by sixteen others. The board was holding a special two-day meeting to plan this move.

It took all of Jefferson's optimism to think he could succeed in changing his little college into an ambitious university. There were serious obstacles in the way, which had baffled earlier efforts to compete with the College of William and Mary (Jefferson's own alma mater); and the obstacles would continue to impede him all through the nine years of struggle toward his goal. Any artist needs means and material to create with. The means often come from a patron, and an artist's foes and friends usually find reason to contest any major act of patronage. This can be especially true for architects—when, for instance, the patron commissioning a work is a corporate body with divided and shifting demands, when funds come in installments, when costs outrun estimates, when members of the commissioning body resign or are replaced. All these things applied to Jefferson's patron, the two chambers of the Virginia state legislature, whose members had conflicting views and whose constituents made conflicting demands. Jefferson needed shrewd and determined allies to deal with this difficult relationship, and he had two who were critical to his success. One was inside the legislature, one outside it, each influential with different segments of the population. The inside man was Joseph Cabell, the outside man John Cocke.

Joseph Cabell, who would labor year after year in the Virginia senate to wrestle installments of funding from the Assembly, was a master strategist who often had to compel Jefferson to take practical steps to protect his idealistic dream. A fellow graduate of William and Mary, Cabell had made the grand tour of Europe, where he met, among other leaders, the education reformer Johann Heinrich Pestalozzi. He would implement some of Pestalozzi's ideas in a ladies' academy he sponsored. Cabell married the wealthiest heiress in Virginia, the daughter of George Carter and granddaughter of Peyton Skipwith. From Cabell's plantation, Edgewood, he promoted reforms and improvements for his state, and served tirelessly in the senate despite ill health. Without him, Jefferson's university could never have got off the ground.

John Cocke's plantation was Bremo, whose great house was built in a distinctively Jeffersonian style by one of the master craftsmen Jefferson had trained, John Neilson (pronounced Nelson). Cocke, known as General Cocke for his rapid promotion during the War of 1812, was a reformer undeterred by Virginians' opposition to his favorite causes—abolitionism, temperance, anti-dueling laws, and agrarian reform. Though many thought Cocke's views utopian, he had a strong practical streak, as one might suspect from his successful wartime service. He had more experience than Jefferson in the running of schools, since he established an academy for boys under fifteen near his plantation, and conducted it with signal results. He was able to use that experience in tempering some of Jefferson's enthusiasms. After Jefferson's death, Cocke tried to rent Monticello to set up a preparatory school for the University of Virginia, but the entanglements of Jefferson's estate made this impossible.

Jefferson had other coadjutors in his great project, but none with the energy, intelligence, and resources of these two. He needed all that they and their friends could offer him, since he had three great obstacles to cope with—religion, money, and local jealousies.

1. RELIGION. Almost all American colleges had been founded by and for religious denominations—Harvard and Yale and Princeton in the colonial period, and over three dozen in the early days of the federal union. Indeed, the competition of religious bodies was what led to the pullulation of small and insufficient establishments. Even the early state schools, like William and Mary itself, had chapels and chaplains. Jefferson had been disgusted by the lazy clergy he encountered during his own college days there, and he tried to reform the school in 1779, when he was governor of the state. But his efforts were resisted, since he was seen by his foes as an enemy of religion. He knew, therefore, that his own scheme of a state school without an establishment of religion would be denounced. He made no provision for a professor of divinity or chaplain. His seventeen

buildings did not include a chapel, though he let it be known that religious bodies could hold student services on their own, so long as none was sponsored by the university itself. This was not enough to end the criticism, and some of his early efforts to recruit professors just exacerbated the problem.

Jefferson was concerned that when the time came to hire a faculty, qualified men would be firmly established where they were, so he decided to snatch at any good man whenever he became available. On the very day after the cornerstone was laid for the first building of Central College, he persuaded a hesitating board to lure the polymath Thomas Cooper from Pennsylvania as the first professor of chemistry. He planned to have the appointment reconfirmed as soon as Central College became the University of Virginia. But Cooper was a friend and disciple of Joseph Priestley, the free-thinking Unitarian driven from England by his sympathy with the French Revolution. Cooper had edited Priestley's works after his mentor's death. Presbyterians in Virginia, frightened of Priestley's reputation, mounted a public campaign against Cooper's appointment. Jefferson privately called these critics "satellites of religious persecution" and insisted that Cooper had been the cornerstone of his whole design. (May 16, 1820) Cabell said that going against Jefferson's strong desire in this matter made him spend sleepless nights and worry himself to the point of a breakdown, but he had to make it clear to Jefferson that this one appointment would sink their whole enterprise. Presbyterians in the legislature had been voting in favor of the new university, out of long discontent with the established Anglicanism of William and Mary. In fact, one of the university's best defenders was the very

Presbyterian, Dr. John H. Rice, who was leading the attack on Cooper. With every vote in the legislature teetering on the possibility of defeat, Cabell said he could not carry the day if Presbyterians deserted him. "I have devoted two winters and one summer of my life to the most sincere cooperation with you in getting this measure through the Assembly. I think I am well apprised of the state of the public mind; and, believe me, the contest is not over." (Feb. 22, 1819) Jefferson had to swallow his pride, spell out the facts to Cooper, and let the latter resign (with a handsome remuneration the university could ill afford).

Cabell taught Jefferson the abiding lesson of this contretemps. Professors should not be appointed one by one, letting people pick over their record and nibble at their qualifications. Jefferson should wait till the end of the building process to make appointments—for two reasons: to present critics with a batch of teachers less easily scrutinized in detail, and to prevent the legislature from cutting off further funds at an early stage after several men had already begun teaching. (C Feb. 22, 1819) Jefferson and the board agreed with this shrewd but risky all-or-nothing approach to the opening of the school; and religion played its part in this decision. Not that this ended religious sniping at Jefferson's scheme. Some Presbyterians circulated the rumor that no clergy, except perhaps Unitarians, would be allowed onto the university's grounds. (C Jan. 7, 1822) The soundness of Cabell's determination to jettison Cooper was proved when Dr. Rice, Cooper's fiercest critic, rallied to knock down the rumor of clergy-free grounds in Charlottesville. Rice went on to perform another important service. He supplied Cabell with a key weapon in the fight for funding the university.

Rice published an estimate of the money Virginians were sending out of the state for the education of their sons in northern colleges, and urged that the money be kept at home.

Jefferson had been aware, from the outset, of the religious opposition to him, and what it might cost him. In the year after work on Pavilion VII had begun, when a state commission was created to decide on the site of a future university, he told Cabell that it would probably hinder their site's effort for him to serve on the commission:

> Would it promote the success of the institution most for me to be in it or out of it? Out of it, I believe. It is still to depend ultimately on the will of the legislature; and that has its uncertainties. There are fanatics both in religion and politics, who, without knowing me personally, have long been taught to consider me as a raw head and bloody bones, and as we can afford to lose no votes in that body, I do think it would be better that you should be named for our district. Do not consider this a mock modesty. It is the cool and deliberate act of my own judgment. (Feb. 26, 1818)

Cabell luckily persuaded Jefferson to put aside his fears and serve on the commission, where his service was crucial to the final choice of a site.

Though Jefferson wanted desperately to complete his university, he could not sacrifice the principle of free enquiry in it, and therefore had to stick to his troublesome resolution to have no divinity taught there.

2. MONEY. Since Jefferson felt that at least ten professors were needed to justify the name of a university, dealing with the entire "circle of the sciences" (Jan. 5, 1815), and since he could not call on organized religion to mobilize the kind of support given to a Harvard or a Yale, his whole plan depended on convincing the legislature to fund a school more ambitious in scale than the one it was already supporting (William and Mary). Here his plan came into opposition with a cause for which he had himself been the principal advocate. At the time of the Revolution, he had proposed an extensive system of public support for primary and secondary education in Virginia. That scheme was only gradually and spottily realized, but it consumed (and indeed strained) most of the budget of the Literary Fund, the state moneys devoted to education of its citizens. Jefferson had argued that the primary schools should be under local control, guaranteed by local funding; but this was unrealistic, since many of the small units he envisaged (divided into "hundreds," according to his theory of "Anglo-Saxon" local democracy) were too poor to provide schools on a level with those in other areas. So critics of the university accused Jefferson of trying to deprive children of basic education in order to create exotic studies for an elite.

When this conflict became acute, Jefferson reversed his stand on the need for local funds to insure local control. He said that money could go to both the primary schools and the university if the secondary schools, funded by the state in his original proposal, were left temporarily (until the university was completed) to shift for themselves:

[The secondary schools] may more conveniently than either of the others be left to private enterprise; 1, because there is a good number of classical schools [that teach Latin] now existing; and 2, because their students are universally sons of parents who can afford to pay for their education. (Jan. 13, 1823)

Later he would reverse himself again, to block the relocation and expansion of the College of William and Mary, by proposing that its funds should be used to establish ten secondary schools throughout the state. This kind of scrimmage activity along shifting lines of conflict would consume his energies year after year, even as he was aging and Cabell's health problems were growing. At each session of the Assembly, the two men had to lobby members and keep arguments for the school before the public by way of reports and planted news stories. Despite Jefferson's belief that there should be a "rotation" of officeholders, he pleaded, sometimes demanded, that university sympathizers in the legislature run again for office in order to keep voting for the needed funds. Cabell even gave him the names of men outside the Assembly who sympathized with the project, so Jefferson could urge them to offer their candidacy for the next session.

Though legislators, even some of those sympathetic to the university, recommended that the plan be implemented in stages, beginning instruction in the first completed buildings and only gradually adding to the faculty and curriculum, Jefferson and Cabell stuck to their decision to plow all money given them entirely into construction, betting that lawmakers would not strand their effort in a state of partial completion. Cabell was emphatic on the subject: "I would use all the disposable funds ... Rapidity of execution is now, I think, of great importance. A quick silent march seems to me the most proper." (G 6.9) Starting small would mean losing the chance to draw a first rate faculty into an entire program of instruction. As Jefferson wrote to Cabell:

> It is not a half-project which is to fill up the enticement of [faculty] character from abroad. To stop where we are is to abandon our high hopes and become suitors to Yale and Harvard for their secondary characters to become our first. Have we been laboring then merely to get up another Hampden-Sidney or Lexington? (Dec. 28, 1822)

Jefferson, though he knew his own time was running out, insisted that the university must hold off its opening until, with all buildings up, it would be "opening largely and in full system." (Dec. 28, 1822) Jefferson's board borrowed heavily for the effort, in the trust that the state would either suspend interest on the loans or remit them entirely.

This game of "chicken" with the funders led to later charges that Jefferson had deceived the Assembly by committing himself to future expenditures not yet authorized. There was more than a modicum of truth to this. But when a newspaper writer accused Jefferson of the practice, he reacted with a rhetoric of outraged innocence:

> He makes me declare that I had intentionally proceeded in a course of dupery of our legislature, teasing them,

as he makes me say, for six or seven sessions, for suc-
cessive aids to the university, and asking a part only at
a time, and intentionally concealing the ultimate cost.
(Feb. 7, 1826)

Jefferson said, truthfully, that he had never actually lied to the
state's representatives; but he and Cabell surely did use every kind
of maneuver short of lying in their struggle to keep the whole
ambitious project afloat. When one of the university's directors of
construction came up with an estimate of what the Rotunda
would cost, Cabell did what he could to suppress the figure:

> Mr. Gordon showed me, on Saturday, a letter which he
> had just received from Mr. Dinsmore, stating that the
> undertakers had ascertained that they could not afford
> to build the library [Rotunda] for less than $70,000.
> At my instance, Mr. Gordon threw the letter in the
> fire. My object was to prevent it from being made an
> improper use of, in the event of its being seen by our
> enemies. (C Dec. 23, 1822)

Cabell had at times to counsel Jefferson against asking too
much from any one session of the Assembly. One year they got
nothing at all. Each year it was touch and go, and each year's
grant was resented by different combinations of regional rivals.

3. LOCAL JEALOUSIES. Friends and alumni of the College of
William and Mary understandably fought the movement to create a new university. They did not want to see their institution

demoted from its dominant position. They argued that it would be better to take what already existed and improve it than to start from scratch elsewhere. Jefferson had long argued that the low malarial site of Williamsburg was unhealthy, and that the place was becoming ever more remote from the mass of the citizenry, which was shifting westward. (These considerations had long ago prevailed in the relocation of the state's capital to Richmond.) But Jefferson's criticism of Williamsburg could recoil upon Charlottesville, since sites even higher up, more clearly salubrious, and farther west, contended that the future belonged to them, in Lexington or Staunton. Thus, in 1818, when the state voted money for a university (an inadequate annual $15,000), it did not say to which locale the funds should go. Central College's first building was already going up, but Washington College had been promised a huge bequest, and Virginians in the Society of the Cincinnati, ardent fans of George Washington, supported the college because it had been established with the help of funds given by the first president. (C Dec. 18, 1817) The town of Staunton, also, was making a powerful effort to found a college.

To determine where its initial grant must go, the Assembly ordered that a special commission should study the merits of the contending sites and meet at Rockfish Gap in the Blue Ridge to formulate a report. The choice of that western venue boded ill for Charlottesville, and so did the decision to let the directors of the Literary Fund choose the commissioners. Cabell, with customary speed of maneuver, got the choice shifted to the governor, James Preston, who came from Albemarle, Jefferson's county. The Literary Fund was left with nothing but the power to fill vacancies if any appointees would not serve:

> The appointment of the commissioners is now a subject of infinite importance to us. The executive, I think, will do us justice. But you will observe that vacancies are to be filled by the president and directors of the Literary Fund. It was proposed, in the committee of the Senate, to give the appointment in the first instance to them. To this I objected, and then it was agreed to give it to the executive. And the fact is that the power left with the president and directors of the Literary Fund was kept in, contrary to my expectation and intention. I relied upon the understanding that the power was to be given to the executive; and, in the hurry of the business, that part of the bill escaped amendment. (C Feb. 22, 1818)

Though Preston favored the Central College site, he was directed to choose one commissioner from each of the state's three dozen or so legislative districts. This meant that the western districts would be outnumbered; but they could call on allies who wanted Jefferson's plan rejected on religious or other grounds. This is the commission Jefferson said he should not serve on, since he would trigger such complaints; but Cabell felt he was needed to mount the case for Albemarle.

Jefferson knew the commission's report would do no good unless he could muster popular and legislative support for it. The report must look like the result of a genuine and free investigation. To give it that air he prepared an elaborate set of calculations to prove that Charlottesville was the true center of the state. His case was accepted by the commission, sixteen of whom voted for Charlottesville and only two each for Lexington and Staunton. (Over a dozen of the commissioners failed to show up at the out-of-the-way meeting place.) After the only contentious issue was settled, that of the site, the commission took up other matters assigned it by the Assembly—the curriculum for the university, the size of its faculty, and the style of its buildings. On all these points Jefferson supplied well-thought-out position papers that were adopted as the official findings.

Though the report was submitted to the legislature in August, Cabell had many months of struggle to get it accepted in both houses. Opponents said that Jefferson had cooked the calculations indicating the center of the state. Cabell relayed Jefferson's arguments, that he had weighted various districts in terms of their density of population. (Jan. 1, 1819) At one point, the committee considering the report was tied, and the chairman had to break the tie in Cabell's favor. Finally, on January 25, 1819, Central College was changed by state law into the University of Virginia. An eloquent plea was made, to those who lost the vote for other sites in the House of Delegates, that all unite for the reputation and progress of Virginia. Cabell told Jefferson that "a great part of the House was in tears" over this address. (C Jan. 18, 1819) But animosities would surface again in later sessions. One battle over, others lay ahead.

The university was to be governed by a Board of Visitors. Jefferson wanted it to be made up of men from the university's immediate region. He argued that this would facilitate more frequent meetings; but he also wanted little if any representation from competing locales. The governor felt that it would not be politically wise to support such a narrow representation, and cast a wider net in his selection of Visitors. This meant there would be at least one man from the area of Staunton, whose bid for the university had been rejected. Cabell advocated for this spot his friend, Chapman Johnson. Not only had he and Johnson been classmates at William and Mary, but they were partners in promoting a canal system for the upper James River that benefited Johnson's region. Cabell assured Jefferson that "no man on the other side of the Ridge could have as much influence in breaking down future opposition from that quarter." (C Feb. 15, 1819)

Johnson, however, had to keep his constituents in mind, and he would prove the most obstructive member of the board—arguing, for instance, against the large sums requested for the Rotunda's completion. (C March 10, 1822) Johnson also attended board meetings irregularly, and Jefferson and Cabell had to send him things to sign in order to keep his appointment from lapsing. They felt he was better than anyone else they could expect from that region. Cabell could usually work with him.

One of Johnson's defections seemed especially dangerous to Jefferson. In 1824, just as the end seemed in sight for the university's construction, there was a move to create a medical school of William and Mary College in Richmond, preparatory to moving the whole school there. Johnson supported this, arguing that it would look as if the university were trying to sabotage another state institution if it opposed a reasonable request. But Jefferson was alarmed that the already exiguous funds coming to his university would dwindle even further and he would be unable to pay his professors enough to retain qualified men. The attempt to make the Williamsburg college a real university would sink his own endeavor. "Few of the states have been able to maintain one university, none two. Surely the legislature, after such an expense incurred for a real university, and just as it is prepared to go into action under hopeful auspices, will not consent to destroy it by this side wind." (Dec. 22, 1824) Cabell agreed on the scale of the danger, "which seems to threaten our total overthrow." (C Dec. 21, 1824) He warned Jefferson of a rumor that Madison, who was a member of the Board of Visitors, had expressed support for the college's move to Richmond. He wanted Jefferson to quash this report if it were false, or to argue Madison out of his position if it were true. (C Dec. 31, 1824) Jefferson's panic gave a shrill edge to his argument that a teaching hospital in Richmond would make no sense. Who would be admitted to it? Hospitals are successful only in cities and ports with transients, sailors, and poor white servants to make up their number of patients. Richmond was not such a place:

> The servants there are slaves, whose masters are by law
> obliged to take care of them in sickness as in health,
> and who could not be admitted into a hospital ... And
> I will ask how many families in Richmond would send
> their husbands, wives, or children to a hospital in sick
> ness—to be attended by nurses hardened by habit
> against the feelings of pity, to lie in public rooms
> harassed by the cries and sufferings of disease under

every form, alarmed by the groans of the dying, exposed as a corpse, to be lectured over by a clinical professor, to be crowded and handled by his students, to hear their case learnedly explained to them, its threatening symptoms developed and its probable termination foreboded? (May 16, 1824)

Jefferson could feel his project being pried from his fingers just when he thought it achieved. To crush this menace he and Cabell resorted to strong-arm tactics. Since the argument for moving William and Mary was that it was not sufficiently performing its task where it was, Cabell introduced a measure to give its budget to ten secondary schools. He and Jefferson proposed ten locales distributed judiciously over electoral districts to recruit support for each by representatives of those regions. Faced with the prospect of losing state support even where it was, the college gave up its plan to move. To save his university, Jefferson was prepared to fight dirty.

The lengths Jefferson would go to had already been demonstrated three years before the threat from William and Mary. He needed a steely resolve to face what he considered as potentially the greatest catastrophe of his long ordeal. In 1821, after nearly five years of struggle for the university, Cabell informed Jefferson that his health would not allow him to make another campaign for his senate seat: "Such is the weakness of my breast that to ride from court house to court house, making speeches to large crowds, exposed to the rigors of the season, might carry me to the grave." (Jan. 25, 1821) Jefferson took this as the death knell of all his hopes. He knew how much he needed Cabell. He could not go on without him. He wrote the most plaintive letter in their whole vast correspondence, accusing Cabell of desertion, "for desertion I must call it." (Jan. 31, 1821) Resorting to emotional blackmail, Jefferson said that he had himself served beyond the limits of most men's endurance, and Cabell must do so as well, even at the cost of his health or his life:

> What object of our lives can we propose so important? What interest of our own which ought not to be postponed [subordinated] to this? Health, time, labor—on what in the single life which nature has given us can these be better bestowed than on this immortal boon to our country? ... Nature will not give you a second life wherein to atone for the omissions of this. Pray then, dear and very dear sir, do not think of deserting us; but view the sacrifices which seem to stand in your way as the lesser duties and such as ought to be postponed to this, the greatest of all.

The ruthlessness of the artist who subordinates everything to his creative task can be cruel on those close to him. How many serene masterpieces have floated improbably up from broken homes, broken health, broken promises? How many betrayals were the price of this great painting or that great symphony? Jefferson did not flinch at sacrificing a friend's peace and content, and possibly his life, if it stood in the way of completing his great work.

He justified himself by noting how much he had already sacrificed himself. Using the term for a Roman soldier's completion of a full forty-year term of military service, he said he had long ago *(iamdudum)* exceeded that:

> If any member of our college of visitors could justifiably withdraw from this sacred duty, it would be myself, who, *quadragenis stipendiis iamdudum peractis,* have neither vigor of body nor mind left to keep the field. But I will die in the last ditch. And so, I hope, you will, my friend.

It is quite true that while Cabell was in legislative harness Jefferson had been coping with problems, breakdowns, shortages, compromises, and disappointments that made his effort seem hopeless from one season to the next. He often couldn't get the workers he wanted. When he got them, he could not keep them for lack of funds or materials. Some of the best craftsmen were alcoholic, and he had to calculate when their failings would cancel their skill. Slaves were able to get to their alcohol, despite the fact that one man was the official dispenser of whisky and rum. When John Cocke promised to send slaves over from his plantation, Bremo, to help with work on the university, they turned out to be boys too small to do heavy lifting. (G 10.2) Workers were jealous of each other and squabbled over who was to do what. An Italian sculptor brought over to carve capitals for the pillars found Virginia stone too friable to be wrought—left with little to do, he hated the food, longed for his young wife back home, and demanded full payment for a curtailed stay. (G 5.6-8) Work suspended in bad weather meant that what was already up was partly ruined by the time work was resumed.

The restraints Jefferson would be working under were clear from the very beginning. The land he wanted to purchase was not for sale. The second best land had a narrower plateau along its ridge than Jefferson had counted on. And though Jefferson wanted his own master builders, James Dinsmore and John Neilson, to start work on Pavilion VII, the man selling the land, John Perry, was a contractor too—he and his brothers had done some work for Jefferson at both his homes, Monticello and Poplar Forest—so Perry made it a condition of the land's sale that he be in charge of the first structure to go up. Not only that. He saw the years of contracts that would be involved in raising the university, and he quickly added to his own holdings in nearby saw mills, brick fields, and ironmonger operations, operated by three dozen or so slaves. Jefferson often had to buy materials from him for easy access and speed of delivery, and that let Perry drive prices up and keep insinuating himself and his relatives as workers. He also controlled the water rights for conduits from nearby property that he still owned.

Jefferson was in continual and often acrimonious negotiation to get materials from Richmond, Philadelphia, and elsewhere at a price he could meet from the state's grudging allotments of cash. He needed slate for fireplaces, tin for roofs, sashes for windows, plaster rosettes, glass. Things came late or not at all. The large capitals for the Rotunda, carved in Italy, were slow to arrive and at first proved too heavy to be carried by boat up the Rivanna River. (G 8.4) To read Frank Grizzard's year-by-year account of the difficulties Jefferson met and surmounted and had to surmount again, repeatedly, is enough to make one wonder how anyone could keep up this endless confrontation with difficulties and disappointments—much less one moving from his late seventies into his early eighties. It is a wonder that we do not hear more often the cri de coeur with which he greeted Cabell's effort to retire: "I perceive that I am not to live to see it [the university] opened." (Jan. 31, 1821) That he did live to see it is a miracle of human determination and artistic ruthlessness.

CHAPTER TWO

New World Artifact

Though Jefferson's university was original in many ways, it was also the fulfillment of a dream long cherished on this continent—the hope for a university fitted to the distinctive American experience, one that would negotiate a new relationship with nature in the New World. European universities had been urban, dotted about in the interstices of a great city like Paris, or monastic, sealed up in gated quadrangles like those at Oxford and Cambridge. American schools, from the very beginning, were open to the countryside, looking out on lawns or greens or yards or "areas"—on the long village mall stretching out before the Wren Building in Williamsburg, or on "the field" (Latin *campus*) before Nassau Hall at the College of New Jersey (later Princeton). Princeton's word for its "campus" would at last be adopted by colleges to indicate their entire plat, but its original meaning shows that our first colleges wanted to address and respond to open space.

The architectural historian Paul Venable Turner argues that college campus planning in the colonial and early Federal period was the most original branch of American architecture, the one that most thoroughly rejected European models. "It has been the laboratory for perhaps the most distinctively American experiments in architectural planning."[1] Many have forgotten how bold was this early period of creativity. They think Gothic quadrangles are America's typical college style; but that fashion did not take hold until the later nineteenth and early twentieth centuries.[2] The first American colleges favored open not enclosed forms and rural rather than urban ones.[3] Even when a university bordered a town's green, as Yale did New Haven's, it sought an expanse of landscape behind the row of buildings— Yale's was planned on an extensive scale by the school's alumnus-artist John Trumbull. Eliphalet Nott, the visionary president of Union College, sold the academy that was the school's first incarnation in the town of Schenectady, to build on a high location with panoramic views of the countryside.

The great prophet of a university for the New World was George Berkeley. Though he is now known as one of the great epistemologists in the eighteenth century, epistemology's golden era, he first became famous for the Enlightenment project of a university to serve the whole of British America from an offshore site in Bermuda. He had a struggle not unlike Jefferson's to get funds from his legislature, lobbying Parliament personally and through friends. As soon as Parliament approved his project, he sailed to America to prepare the recruitment of students and resources. Meanwhile, back in London, opponents of his project killed its funding in his absence. (He did not have a Joseph Cabell fighting in the bowels of the legislature, as Jefferson did.) Nonetheless, Berkeley had a great influence on American schools during the three years he spent in New England (1729-1731). He sought and gave advice on university education with the faculties of Harvard, Yale, and King's College (Columbia). His association with Yale was especially close. He left to its library the books he had been collecting for Bermuda, and bequeathed to the school the home he had built in Newport, Rhode Island. One of Yale's residential colleges is named Berkeley in his honor, and a graduate of that college who admired its namesake founded the Berkeley branch of the University of California.

Berkeley wanted to establish his school in Bermuda for several reasons—to build on virgin soil, to avoid the provincialism of any one colony in North America, to draw Native Americans to the school. Berkeley believed in a direct access to ideas through nature, and he wanted a fresh start for knowledge, unencumbered by old prejudices. His plan for the buildings, widely published and discussed, anticipated some of the ideal architecture of France that would later impress Jefferson. The buildings were to be arranged in two concentric circles around an "omphalos," the chapel (Berkeley was an Enlightenment philosopher but also a parson—he would become a bishop on his return to England). The inmost concentric circle of the university was to hold the faculty residences and classrooms, the outermost one the student dwellings and services. There was a cosmic hierarchy reflected in these spheres, which were open to the world on all sides. A model town was to be built nearby to provide the port for trafficking in students and goods. It was a tremendously ambitious scheme, which came close to realization despite its ideal nature, so hard and long did Berkeley work at it. This grand failure resembles what could have happened to Jefferson's project if, at any one of numerous crises, it had been blocked—as it almost was.

That Jefferson was drawn to the Berkeley ideal can be seen from the fact that he approved a variant of it, proposed for a national university in 1799, when Jefferson was vice president of the United States and president of the American Philosophical Society. In the latter capacity, he chaired a committee judging a contest proposed by the Society for the layout of a national university. Samuel Knox won the prize, with a variant of Berkeley's plan, one with concentric squares of buildings rather than concentric circles. Knox put a rotunda-observatory at the center of his plan instead of a chapel, and placed the faculty in the outer (not the inner) square. But the plan had the same omnidirectional contact with nature as did Berkeley's.

Jefferson was, from his youth, widely known to be interested in university planning and improvement. When he was still in his twenties, Virginia's royal governor, Lord Dunmore, asked him to draw up a plan for expanding the Wren Building that housed the College of William and Mary. Later, Jefferson was consulted by two Frenchmen who tried to solder the Franco-American alliance with plans for French universities in America—by Alexandre Marie Quesnay, Chevalier de Beaurepaire in 1799 (Quesnay succeeded in raising one building for his project in Richmond), and then by Pierre-Samuel du Pont de Nemours in 1800. In 1804 Jefferson drew up a first version of his "academical village" at the request of a member of the Virginia House of Delegates, and in 1810 he forwarded an improved sketch of it to the trustees of a proposed university in Tennessee.

Robert Mills, the later planner of the Washington Monument, was doing his architectural apprentice work with Jefferson when he submitted a plan to the first college competition in this country (for the College of South Carolina in 1802). His design was chosen over that of Latrobe, whose workshop he was about to enter. The design was not built, but it proposed the first covered arcade connecting classroom entrances in the history of American schools—a feature Jefferson would later use for his university's ranges and would adapt (as a colonnade) for the Lawn. (Mills himself returned to Charlottesville in 1852 to build an Annex to Jefferson's Rotunda.)

While some were consulting Jefferson on plans for universities, he kept an eye on others' proposals and achievements. He would have known Joseph Jacques Ramée's stunning design for Union College, published in 1813. This resembled Berkeley's plan in that it had a central chapel with a semicircle of buildings around it. Instead of closing the circle, however, Ramée ran wings from both ends of its open ends (FIGURE 9). The scheme combines maximum openness to nature with maximum order and self-reference of all the parts to one another—the very qualities Jefferson would develop in his own way at Charlottesville.

But the major figure in Jefferson's study of university architecture was Benjamin Latrobe, with whom Jefferson had worked closely on the construction of the federal city. Latrobe was the most sought-after and experienced university architect. When Nassau Hall at Princeton burned down, it was he who rebuilt it,

FIGURE 9. *Ramée's plan for Union College*

improving its design in the process. He then designed the Hall's flanking buildings, Stanhope Hall and Philosophical Hall. In Philadelphia he altered the old federal executive mansion to become the University of Pennsylvania. Altogether he laid out or did work on eight campuses, and drew up designs for a national university and for a military academy. Neither of these last two was built, but Jefferson knew of them and probably discussed them with the American architect he most respected. Latrobe's military academy has a U-shaped plan with a central dome on its base leg. Though it is a single building, and is sealed off at the open end of the U by a sentry-gate for military security, certain of its aspects resemble Jefferson's plan for Charlottesville. Faculty residences are intermingled with those of the students. Strikingly, there is no chapel (FIGURE 10).

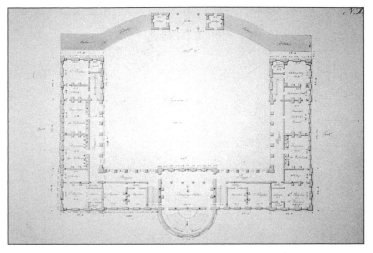

FIGURE 10. *Latrobe's plan for a military academy*

Jefferson had thus been given many decades to reflect on the needs of faculty and students in an American institution of higher learning. He knew what he liked and disliked in the models available to him. He accepted the relationship to nature that other schools aspired to. But he emphatically rejected the idea of beginning with a single building that would hold all the school's activities—as had been the case with Nassau Hall and the Wren Building. These structures, he knew from experience, were noisy, unhealthy, vulnerable to fires, and affording little privacy. He proposed instead a cluster of smaller buildings, what he called "an academical village." The buildings should not be scattered randomly about, but should be interrelated in ways that symbolize the whole endeavor. As he completed his thoughts on the matter, he played off a large communal library against individual residences for the faculty, each such "Pavilion" containing a classroom dedicated to that teacher's field, and students' rooms interspersed between the faculty buildings.

Every Pavilion, though it faces out on a level public Lawn, would have a private walled garden on the declivity behind it. Hotels lay just beyond these gardens, with more rows of student dormitories connecting them, just as they connect the Pavilions on the Lawn. These Hotels, three to each side of the plan, were to provide eating facilities for the students, along with other services (laundry, supplies, servants to clean their rooms). Each Hotel had its own kitchen garden carved out of the proximate professor's garden. Traffic flow, weather conditions, exercise areas, laboratories, stabling facilities, a nearby observatory on a height—all were given consideration and assigned a place in Jefferson's scheme. Yet the whole is not over-regimented. The effect is of disciplined freedom. Jefferson avoided the oversimplified outline of Berkeley's plan, or Samuel Knox's. But in articulating parts of different scale and purpose, the plan did not succumb to the mere scatter of the original Harvard Yard, the mere straggle of the Yale Row.

The separation of the main buildings into ten units reflected Jefferson's long pondering of "the sciences useful in our time." After drawing up many stemmata of the branches of learning, he decided that an irreducible minimum of ten was needed to be adequate to the growth of knowledge in his day. That is why he resisted so energetically any effort to start the university with a few buildings and professors. It was the interaction of the *whole* realm of learning that was essential to his vision. Anything less than that was unworthy of the name "university."

To suggest the relationships involved in the buildings, he needed the widest range of differentiating symbols, some suggesting hierarchy, some equality.

The Rotunda, meant to hold the library and certain communal functions, towers over the ten teaching quarters (FIGURE 14, p. 78). It has Corinthian columns, the most dignified, on its exterior, but Doric, Ionic, and Composite ones in various parts of the interior. This was meant to convey the comprehensiveness of the central storehouse of knowledge. When Jefferson asked the architect of the United States Capitol, William Thornton, to offer suggestions for the university, Thornton advised him against using Composite capitals, since they were a modern invention, not truly classical. But Jefferson wanted to incorporate some modern elements in his design (notably in Pavilion IX. FIGURE 7, p. 15).

The Pavilions themselves conform, singly, to one or other of the three main orders (Doric, Ionic, Corinthian), but the buildings are artfully individualized to guarantee that no single Pavilion is stylistically superior to another. There was to be no hierarchy of academic disciplines, as in Old World universities where theology was "queen of the sciences." The Pavilions' placement on the Lawn is not meant to suggest gradations of dignity, and professors were originally assigned to their Pavilions by the drawing of lots.

Jefferson's determination to make the Pavilions equal would have been even more obvious if he had stuck to his original plan for them. He first envisioned classical orders (of columns and entablatures) only on the second stories, the living quarters of the professors. The lower stories, with classrooms, would simply have the colonnade (originally, the arcade) running across them—as at the original building, Pavilion VII

FIGURE 11. *Pavilion III*

(FIGURE 4, p. 12). But Latrobe suggested putting "colossal" orders on some of them—columns running up past both the first and second stories. To do this, Jefferson seized the opportunity to advance such columns out onto the Lawn, outside the run of the little Tuscan colonnade. On Pavilion III, for instance, the columns advance out from their own building's side bays, out beyond the deck on its second story, interrupting the flow of Tuscan columns entirely (FIGURE 11). This admirably varied the relationships of colonnade and Pavilions. He put five of these colossal orders near the Rotunda, easing the transition to its huge Corinthian columns—though he gave one of the terminal Pavilions (X) its own colossal order (FIGURE 8, p. 16).

To avoid making the colossal Pavilions superior to the others, Jefferson cleverly mixed the elements of them all—

doors, parapets, "wings" extending beyond the architrave, balconies, projections, recesses—to prevent any system of grading by a single measure. Some Pavilions (both the double-tiered and the colossal) have four columns (tetrastyle), one has six (hexastyle), with neither ranking above the other. He wanted to stress the dignity of each separate branch of knowledge taught in the Pavilions, and he did not associate any one place with one discipline. There were no signs of *what* was to be taught within.

The dialogue between branches of knowledge is suggested by the upper-level walkway between the Pavilions, letting professor commune with professor above traffic at the Lawn level. This is the physical expression of an ideal he set for composing the faculty.

> We are next to observe that a man is not qualified for a professor [by] knowing nothing but merely his own profession. He should be otherwise well educated as to the sciences generally; able to converse understandingly with the scientific men with whom he is associated, and to assist in the councils of the faculty on any subject of science on which they may have occasion to deliberate. Without this, he will incur their contempt and bring disreputation on the institution. (Feb. 23, 1824)

This communication "on the higher level" is informal and casual, not scheduled and constant, so the walkways above are not covered, like the colonnade connecting the Pavilions at ground level, "under which they [the students] may go dry from school to school." (June 12, 1817)

Thornton advised Jefferson to use little columns, not square piers, to connect the Pavilions by means of these walkways; but he warned against using Tuscan columns, since they are only "a very clumsy Doric" form. Jefferson, however, wanted to extend his range of differentiating elements. He had already reserved square brick piers for the walkways along the outer ranges, which are more rustic than the formalities of the Lawn (FIGURES 2 AND 3, pp. 10-11). He needed a step up from those that would still be a step below the small Doric columns used on two-tiered (non-colossal) Pavilions. The Tuscan columns of the Lawn's colonnade are modest. They provide a ground bass for the melodic traceries of the Pavilion facades. He wanted something neither too obtrusive nor too meager for these columns. Their light color forms a perfect contrast with the redbrick piers in the lower ranges. They were not originally white—on this, too, Jefferson took Thornton's advice, making them a light earthen color.

It is often said that, before the Lawn was sealed off by the later buildings at its southern end, Jefferson envisaged the indefinite extension of it outward by the addition of new Pavilions. It is true that he advised the Tennessee university planners that they might start their rows of buildings with such additions in mind, and his own first drawing of the university's layout had dots suggesting an extension of that sort. But that drawing had only three professors' buildings on either side. Once he settled on five, he would not have wanted the distance from the library to be made too great for students and faculty living at the farther end of such an expansible telescope. He certainly did see the first seventeen structures as a nucleus around which new elements would be organized. But he provided for this development by the addition of new rows of buildings to flank the Ranges. This would change his plan from one of four parallel rows of buildings to one of six (or, eventually, eight, ten, and so on).

He began one new row in alignment with the east Range by constructing stables for the professors. To initiate a similar row along the west Range, he placed there his Anatomical Theater for the professor of medicine to perform dissections in. His decision to add this building to his original scheme was no doubt influenced by the threat of a hospital to be established by the College of William and Mary in Richmond. Advocates of that scheme had said that Jefferson's university would teach only medical history, not medical practice. Stung by that challenge, Jefferson studied the nature of a building for the performance of dissections. When the first professor of medicine arrived (Robley Dunglison), he made it clear that he meant to perform autopsies, and that he could not do it in the classroom for Pavilion X, under his wife's bedroom.

The first floor admitted light through semicircular windows, raised above eye level so that voyeurs could not see the anatomical displays on the first floor. Stairways in the corners of the building led up to the dissection theater on the second floor. The small triangular spaces taken up by the corner stairs made it possible for Jefferson to use his favorite octagonal shape for the tiers of students rising all around the central dissecting table (FIGURE 12). Semicircular windows were placed on this floor too, to let in light from all directions, supplementing the flood of illumination from a skylight. Construction of the building began before Jefferson's death but

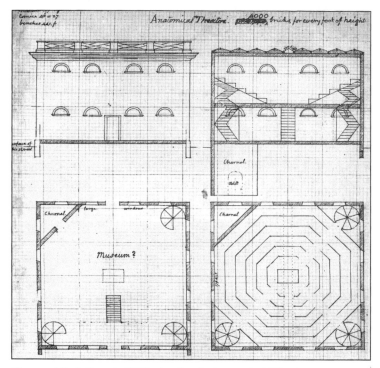

FIGURE 12. *Jefferson's 1825 plan for the Anatomical Theater*

was completed only after it, and it is the only major structure he designed for the place that has been destroyed (in 1938, to make room for the new library).

One of the new buildings Jefferson had in mind would be dedicated to the fine arts, including architecture. That had been included in some of his earlier lists of disciplines to be taught; but instead of making another Pavilion for this subject, adding it to the ten Pavilions marching down the Lawn, he would probably have made a cluster of studios on a professional level with the anatomical theater (and aligned with it). He had other laboratory-type additions in mind, including one for his beloved science of agriculture, but the place for them was on the flanks of the Ranges, closer to the library (in the Rotunda) than if they had straggled out to the south. The visual unity of the Lawn was very important to him.

He wanted to make of the whole university a complex teaching machine, with parts interrelated as in David Rittenhouses's "orerry" (model of the universe), which he admired so much. The orders on the Pavilions were chosen from the most chaste and "correct" ancient examples, so they could be used to instruct students in the different styles and their sources, in Roman temples and civic buildings, "furnishing to the student examples of the precepts he will be taught." (April 2, 1816) He even asked the government to remit duties for the import of huge Corinthian capitals from Italy on the grounds that they were educational materials, "a just encouragement to science."[4] Sometimes this effort to make every part function didactically could go to almost comic lengths. He thought of hiring ethnic couples to run the Hotels (eating clubs) for the students, so they would hear them speaking French or Italian or other languages and learn more from them if they desired to.

He also thought of making the interior surface of the Rotunda dome an astronomical display space, with a professor riding a boom to point out the relationships of the planets as they were reconfigured—another large-scale projection of the orerry.[5] Even his serpentine walls around the gardens were meant to have a teaching function—aesthetically, as exemplifying Hogarth's line of grace and beauty; and in physics, since they demonstrate that a wall one brick thick will stand if (and only if) it is curved.

Even some of Jefferson's admirers thought that he tried to pack too many functions into his scheme, that there was not sufficient room for all he was trying to do. Thornton and Latrobe, the architects he asked for advice, both told him that the professors were not given much breathing space, since they were to be provided with only two rooms on the upper floor of a Pavilion, with a basement for their kitchen. (They did not mention, perhaps did not realize, that such a kitchen would be tended by a live-in slave—the professors' basements would be at least as ample as the cook's room recently restored at Jefferson's much larger establishment at Monticello.) Several on the Board of Visitors would join in this criticism, including John Cocke, Chapman Johnson, and even Joseph Cabell.

But Jefferson did not want to change the proportions established for the Pavilions, with the Rotunda on the next scale up and the student dormitories on the next scale down. Increasing the size of the Pavilions would throw off the visually pleasing hierarchy of relationships, each of which was calibrated in terms of all the others. Jefferson had already proved at Monticello that he would sacrifice practicality for aesthetic effect. But he did provide for three or four rooms upstairs, and he assured Latrobe that he would leave the back walls of the Pavilions without windows, so extensions could be built out from them, using the full three stories of the buildings on that side. One of the first professors immediately began such an extension, without waiting for authorization, and all the Pavilions but one have followed that example in the course of the university's later life.

Jefferson's effort was vindicated in the long run. The proportions are preserved on the Lawn, and living quarters have been developed in various ways. Of course, most professors now inhabit the whole house—only one of the original classrooms on the first floor is still used for that purpose. For a while, some professors took over the two student "dormitories" adjacent to their house on either side. But those have been restored to their original purposes. The faculty homes, with necessary additions like indoor plumbing and electricity, are highly desirable to this day, and only such privileged members as deans are rewarded with the right to live in them.

John Cocke, who had experience with students and teachers in his own academy, objected also to the student dormitories and the Hotels along the Ranges. He thought the little cells, originally designed to have two students in each, would be isolated and lonely, as well as too cold in winter and too hot in summer. There were windows only at the back, so the front door would have to be opened to get air—and that would expose the students to the walkway traffic right on their doorstep. In a way, Cocke was right. I interviewed a number of students living on the Lawn in the spring of 2002. They admitted that it is hard for them to have privacy in warm weather, with students swarming on the Lawn, just outside their open doors. Some say they just close up their room at such times (there is only one student per cell now) and go to the library or some other place to get their work done.

On the other hand, in the winter or at night they have an opposite problem—loneliness. The Lawn is spectral, the other cells are sealed up, with no light visible from their windowless front walls under the colonnade. Students must go out of their rooms, travel down the walkway to a gap in the run of dormitories, and descend stairs to the back area where toilets and showers are—a cold trip in winter. Black students were admitted to the Lawn (in the 1960s) before women students (in the 1970s) because of what feminists know as "the bathroom problem." It was said that no new bathrooms and showers could be created for the women—who would not, in any case, make the long cold trip to them in their bathrobes. When I interviewed students on the Lawn, there were more women than men there, and none had been deterred by cold trips to the shower.

In fact I could not find anyone, male or female, who regretted having bid for the honor of living where they do for one (their senior) year. To win a place, they must submit applications to a screening board, presenting their academic qualifications and their record of service to the university. There is an extraordinary camaraderie among those who take the lodgings "Mr. Jefferson" designed for them. This is felt not only by those living on the Lawn at any one time. It is a social tie felt across the generations. One woman student told me she had been visited by dozens of former inhabitants of her room, sharing the privilege of having spent their senior year at that number (as the rooms are called).

Though Jefferson consigned his students to uniform cells, this was meant to set them apart, not to reduce them to cogs in his teaching machine. In fact, he left them an extraordinary degree of freedom in the choice of what they would learn, and from whom. That, too, is what makes this a New World institution. Though Jefferson crafted the range of subjects the school would teach to Americans wanting to acquire "sciences useful to them," he arranged their tuition charges in such a way that they could create their own study program. Simultaneously, this system offered incentive to the faculty to make their courses attractive to the students and competitive with those being offered by other professors. Each faculty member was given a base payment by the school, to be supplemented from students voluntarily choosing which professor or professors to study with. If a student chose only one, he paid that man fifty dollars for the year. If two, the student paid each man thirty dollars; if three or more, twenty-five dollars to each. The man being paid fifty dollars would be expected to give proportionally greater attention to the one doing all his work with him. The others would have to perform in such a way that they too would be candidates for the full tuition as students came to know their work. This presumed that the students were capable of informed decisions about their own needs—with counseling, of course, whenever they sought it.

Jefferson liked this rational-chooser system so well that he set up a free enterprise system for the Hotels as well. These would be given to independent entrepreneurs, husband-and-wife teams, who would compete for students' fees by offering good service. A student could shop around for the best food available, the best supplies offered, the most conscientious servants employed. If any Hotel excelled so clearly in its combination of services offered as to reach its capacity of students enrolled, the other Hotels would have to compete for the spillover. If any Hotel proved so inadequate that students shunned it, then a new couple would have to be brought in to run it.

By providing a mixture of central control, faculty supervision, private enterprise, and individual initiative, Jefferson tried to create a kind of "federalism" of divided functions and responsibilities. The board, and Jefferson as its rector, would have ultimate oversight; but it would turn over actual operation to different agents in different spheres. It was a noble dream, but it soon ran up against intractable realities. Jefferson had counted too much on the maturity of the students and the integrity of the hoteliers. Drastic changes in this aspect of the plan had to be taken, as we shall see. More regulation was needed, as in the larger world, precisely to protect freedom of action. But the spirit of the place still breathes from the very ensemble of its buildings. The student body at Charlottesville has been encouraged, more than most, to be self-governing. The symbolism of a Jeffersonian attitude is encapsulated in, but not confined to, the students who fill the Lawn, a new crop of them every year. They tend to be super-achievers—television's Katie Couric was the head resident (elected leader) of the Lawn in the 1970s. But despite the individual ambition of these students, they are chosen also on the basis of service to the community. A *cooperative* competitiveness does express the spirit Jefferson hoped to find in his students. That has not always been the case. The school has gone through some very dark periods. But the Jeffersonian spirit can always be regenerated from the very fact that its physical expression is so legible.

Even students and faculty who do not live on the Lawn or in the Ranges, those who attend the much larger university that has grown up around them, or who populate the allied professional schools, think of the Lawn as the soul of the place. Great events take place there, formal receptions, rallies, commencements. There is a constant running up and down the scales of form and function as one places oneself in various parts of that inner complex of buildings and their connections. John Donne wrote, "I am a little world made cunningly," a microcosmic echo of the whole vast cosmos. The university is an intermediate cosmic system, housing the microcosmic individuals who are absorbing the lessons of the macrocosm. Despite any changes, over the years, in what or how or where people have been taught, *as an artifact* the first cluster of buildings continues to teach the meaning of teaching.

CHAPTER THREE

Dialogue with Nature

The mission control center during the nine years of construction at the university was Jefferson's plantation on the little mountain above its site. The link between the two was not accidental. Jefferson had for years tried to attract scholars and pupils to a seat of learning near his home. Though he enjoyed the romantic sublime of his isolated perch, he often felt starved for intellectual stimulation. He invited learned men to visit for long periods—the Abbé Jose, Correa da Serra, founder of the Portuguese Academy of Sciences and a member of the Royal Society of England, was there so often that one bedroom was known as "the Abbé's room." During the Revolution, Jefferson invited certain captured British officers, interned in Charlottesville, to come up and dine with him on the mountain, providing intellectual discussion for his table. Before he was forced by debt to sell his books to the Library of Congress, he used the promise of donating them as a lure to bring a college to his vicinity. He petitioned President Washington to raise funds to transport dissident Swiss professors to Virginia, since they could provide the core of a future university. (Washington, who realized that French-speaking academicians would be more useful to Jefferson than to young Virginia students, turned down the request.)

When at last, after long effort, Jefferson managed to combine funds and land (both exiguous at first) for a university at the foot of his plantation-eyrie, he was able to oversee it daily, even while running the farms that provided his living. From Monticello's north terrace, he could see whether work was being done below by training his telescope on the site—and workers knew that his superintending intellect always had them under survey. In the early years of building, he rode his horse down the mountainside, to take a closer look and redirect his master workers' efforts, every other day on average (weather permitting). As time went on and age took its toll, he sometimes had to be carried down in his carriage (more jolting than travel by horseback but with others doing the physical work). At last he became too feeble for carriages, too, and asked the proctor (overseer) of the project and some master workmen to come up to him for progress reports and instructions. When the Marquis de Lafayette came to Charlottesville in 1824, during his famous visit to America, Jefferson was able to make it down to the university to show the distinguished guest around, as well as to attend a banquet in the Marquis's honor inside the partly finished Rotunda. But when Lafayette came back nine months later, toward the end of his tour, Jefferson had to send words down to the banquet that was again held for Lafayette in the Rotunda.

Monticello was not simply an observation post for the building of the university. It was in effect the soul of the larger fabric going up within its sphere of influence. There have been many attempts to assign a principal model for the university complex. One of the most commonly cited influences is the line of lodges down a central mall at the royal French residence Marly—as if , Jefferson could consciously make a monarch's pleasure retreat his pattern. Other universities, as we have seen, had something of the spirit of Jefferson's institution. So did the villas of Palladio, which Jefferson called "ornamented farms." But the latter comparison just points to the connection with Jefferson's own farm, derived in part from Palladio. The real model for the university is the plantation to which it responds in a kind of architectural conversation. The World Heritage Convention was right to place them together as a single treasure.

It may seem perverse to say that a domestic building was the model for a public institution. But a plantation of any size in Virginia was a kind of "agricultural village," analogous to the multiple-but-related activities of Jefferson's "academical village." The plantation, too, contained an orderly arrangement of buildings. There was a central cluster, the great house with two or more flanking buildings (called dependencies). The great house usually faced out on a spacious lawn above a boat landing on the river. (Most plantations were sited on a river large enough to ferry the farms' hogsheads of tobacco out to oceangoing vessels, which could move them across to Europe, mainly to Scotland.) Behind the great house, less visible from the river and the formal lawn, were rows of buildings, often arranged around formal and vegetable gardens, along with water wells, icehouses, and a network of privies designated for use by the different classes of residents and workers living in or near the great house. The number and function of outlying structures varied according to the state of each plantation, but they could include things like stables, carriage houses, laundry huts, smokehouses, roofed butchering areas, orangeries for growing fruits and vegetables in forced heat, manufactures for shoes and clothes made to meet the slaves' needs, carpenter's sheds for tools and workspace in foul weather, ironmonger or blacksmith quarters for making and repairing tools, and so on. Then, farther out on the periphery of this microcosm, were the slave quarters, the pigs for making ham and bacon, the places for wagons, plows, and large equipment. Since surviving great houses have lost all or most of their peripheral structures, we tend to think of them merely as homes rather than as the busy hub of large-scale agricultural enterprises.

Monticello had at one time many of the plantation buildings mentioned, along with things special to it (like a nail factory for Jefferson's own and his neighbors' architectural projects). Jefferson's design and Monticello's site made many of the working functions nearly invisible, neatly tucked into the sloping ground. In the many years he spent creating the great house, he could alter the customary relations of such a house to its site, since he built on a mountain top rather than a river side. He defied economic sense for his aesthetic purpose, which was to have an observed and observing perch in the clouds. He regretted that the small plateau on the top of the mountain did not let him lay out an extensive series of gardens in the English manner. For that reason, his university could not be built on the top and sides of a mountain. Its layout was more complex in its traffic patterns than any (even the largest) English garden.

Despite such necessary differences in the two "villages," there are basic points of similarity in the sites, and in Jefferson's treatment of the sites. He built his university along a ridge with declivities on either side. His home stands on a mountain top with steep plunges on all sides. He meant to make the topography in both cases work for his own purpose. To do so, he had to adjust his first abstract designs, making his work hug the ground, working its resistances into advantages, engaging every building in a dialogue with its terrain, with what he called "the law of the land."

Jefferson's first design for his great house emphasized the height it stood on. The building pulled itself up and away from its surroundings. It was modeled on a Palladian villa that was suburban, as vertical as the contiguous city wall of Montagnana. But his stay in France converted him to more horizontal designs. He realized that he could make the house reach out to its surroundings but still make it the crowning element in his agricultural context. The sunken "offices" under his terrace cleared the view toward his house. The dependencies at the end of each terrace perform an ornamental function, as punctuation points on either side of the garden. They also serve a "propylaia" (sacral gateway) purpose as one approaches the Jeffersonian "acropolis" (hill city). Coming up on the dependencies from the far slope on either side, one reads the white gable ends as minor "rhymings" with the white pediment over the west portico (FIGURE 13).

FIGURE 13. *Monticello's north pavilion and west portico*

When Jefferson lowered the profile of the house, he made it porous to its surroundings. Nature strides into it from all sides and strikes down on it through many skylights. The house bulges out toward its setting in semi-octagonal extrusions on three sides. On the fourth side, the house invites nature into a recessed entry, seen through earth-colored columns. In this recessed portico, there are rusticated panels of imitation stone under the windows. The slates under foot are gray-green, leading in to the grass-green floor of the hall, which provides a proper setting for a museum of natural history. Real grass grows on the top of the steps on the other side of the house. The arcades at either end have a rough finish, and the rows of triple-sashed windows behind their open arches can be thrown up to make so many doors in a breeze walk. The place could not be more welcoming to circumambient air and light. The octagon parlor has three projecting walls filled with tall rows of windows. On Jefferson's private side of the house is a greenhouse flanked by shuttered areas that are neither inside nor outside the structure proper.

This negotiation of a conversation between the inner and outer worlds is continued out onto and beyond the lawn. The great house's classical colonnade communicates with a romantic garden, modeled in its small scale on English asymmetries. The long loose walk around its edges is based on Hogarth's curving "line of grace and beauty," and it repeats on this upper level the lariat-loops of the "roundabouts" by which Jefferson tiered the approach to his peak. These stages of ascent were to run through reshaped forest as a kind of natural garden with vistas to make up for the long level views of an English estate. After all, Jefferson had better scenery to offer from his home's height. And, as the English did, he meant to lead on and tease the eye by the use of exotic little temples or rustic markers, pointing toward planned glimpses of things in the distance.

> Of prospect I have a rich profusion and offering itself
> at every point of the compass. Mountains distant and
> near, smooth and shaggy, single and in ridges, a little
> river hiding itself among the hills so as to show in
> lagoons only, cultivated grounds under the eye and
> two small villages ... To prevent a satiety of this
> [boundless prospect] is the principal difficulty. It may
> be successively offered, and in different portions,

through vistas, or—which will be better—between thickets so disposed as to serve as vistas, with the advantage of shifting the scenes as you advance on your way. (July, 1806)

For his whole conception, therefore, Jefferson graded artistic control out from the great house and down along the flanks of the mountain, so it would fade imperceptibly out into the untouched grandeur of surrounding sky, fields, and forests.

At the summit was a house that was no longer just the Palladian exercise it began as. Jefferson apologized to Latrobe, when he invited him to visit Monticello, for the home's "inaccuracies"—which is ironic, since Latrobe had criticized Jefferson for his reliance on classical "authorities" for every feature of the buildings in Washington. What Jefferson's process of building and rebuilding forced on him was superior to what any simple and more consistent plan would have been. Purists can object that the exterior, seen from different angles, gives no sense of the overall footprint of the house, or of the distribution of its interior spaces. It plays peekaboo with the viewer. It seems smaller than it is because its parts telescope out to narrow arcades at either end. The illusion of a two-story height is created on the east side by putting the second-story windows down at floor level, as if they were extensions of the lights below. The dome has no interior use. It is "simply ornamental." But it provides an ordinating point for the whole plantation. It also suggests the round top of the mountain we are standing on. By sinking and subordinating so many of the outworks, Jefferson made sure that his house, despite its horizontal lines, would still be seen as the culmination of the whole plantation. It is interesting that one of his favorite models of domed buildings, the Villa Rotonda of Palladio, also has no practical interior use for the great height of its dome. It is meant for exterior command of the building's own flanks and its surrounding countryside.[1]

There can never be another Monticello—a building that is ancient and modern, regular and irregular, classical and romantic, formal and informal, efficient and impractical. No other building in the world reflects more completely the mind of the man who built it, his relation to the land that upholds it, his combination of the scholarly and the quotidian. The difference between Jefferson's first plan and his completed building is like the difference between Palladio's plans for his villas in *The Four Books of Architecture* and the actual villas that he raised in the Veneto—except that the plans came first in Jefferson's case, while Palladio's plans were drawn up after he had built the actual villas. What Palladio offered on the page was a utopian set of ideal forms. He completed projects that topography, shortage of funds, or the whim of his patrons had made him curtail or alter. There was no room for the perfect symmetry of responsive parts that he taught in his treatise. But some architecture scholars think that Palladio may have sold himself short in *The Four Books.* His taste and ingenuity as an architect emerge most strikingly in the solutions he found to practical obstacles as he created his material artifacts.[2] The same can be said of Jefferson's achievements on the ground, however "inaccurate" they were according to his own theoretical presuppositions. This is as true of the university as it is of Monticello.

FIGURE 14. *The Rotunda*

Jefferson's first plan for the university quickly ran into practical difficulties. He first drew its Lawn as the three sides of an open square, each of the three lengths of it containing three Pavilions. When he sent a sketch of this plan to Latrobe, the latter suggested that a large central building be substituted for the middle Pavilion on the base of the U-shape. By the time when Jefferson had to cope with the narrower ridge he was able to buy, he was left with room for only one building on what was now the north (short) end of a rectangular space. Making that one building a commanding presence at the end of an allée was now the obvious choice. The Rotunda all but raised itself from the exigencies of the space.

The architectural critic Lewis Mumford thought Jefferson made the main building *too* commanding. In a treatment of the university that is highly admiring in general, he finds the only fault in the height of the Rotunda and its huge portico (FIGURE 14). He judged that they are out of scale with the Pavilions.[3] But Jefferson meant the dome of the building to be visible not only from the Lawn. Before the growth of tall buildings in the modern town and university, it was an ordinating landmark giving the whole university its central position in the valley where it stands. More especially, the partial glimpses given of the dome from the Ranges and gardens is the only indication that there is a central sector of the whole complex. It indicates that the backs of the Pavilions are not a single row of buildings but stand in subordination to some higher entity above and beyond them.

The relationship of the Rotunda to its flanking Pavilions resembles that of Monticello's great house to the arms reaching out toward its dependencies. The row of offices underneath the Monticello terraces resembles the low run of the students' rooms connecting the elements on the university Lawn (FIGURE 15). Jefferson repeated the irregular loop of his garden walk in the roundabouts lower down on the mountain, and he circumscribes the descending gardens of the university in serpentine walls. The more intimate one's experience of the one place becomes, the more its ties to the other reveal themselves. This would be even truer, of course, if various ancillary buildings existed on the fringes of the main plan—the pig stalls for instance, that supplied the smokehouses in both places. (G 10.9)

What impresses, in both places, is the dialogue with the terrain. It was noticed in the Prologue how the dropping down of the Lawn in two places to form three tiers of land made for creative irregularities in the run of the Tuscan columns, which

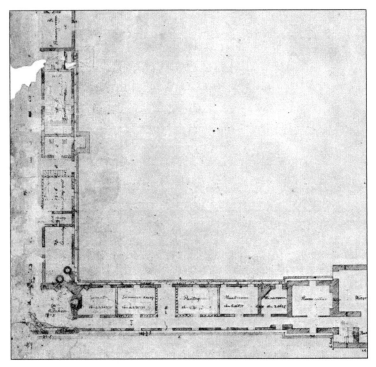

FIGURE 15. *Jefferson's late-eighteenth century plan of Monticello*

also had to be adjusted to the different projections of the Pavilions' porticos. The Pavilions had to adjust their rear facades to different levels and configurations of the ground behind them, where their three-story height is revealed. (Basements are hidden on the Lawn side.)

If the play of particular adaptation against overall pattern is subtly evident on the Lawn, it is dramatically obtrusive on the flanks of the Lawn falling off toward the Ranges, where

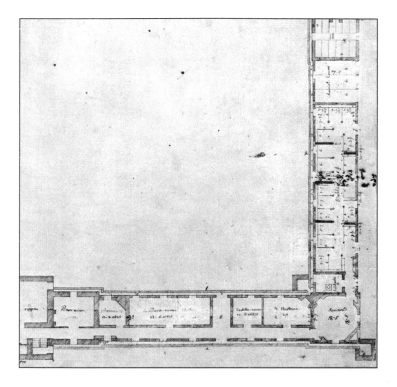

declivities and undulations jumble the patterns without destroying them. Grading smoothed out some of the unevenness with which the land falls away on either side; but the main effort was to use the land creatively. The proctor of the project, Brockenbrough, found that he could not easily fit the Hotels into their allotted spaces. They had to be moved out a few feet to get firm footing on the west side, and they were moved out even farther on the steeper east side—which means that the gardens are wider on that side. Where to place the "roads" on either side also presented a problem. These were needed for carts to bring wood and other supplies to the Pavilions, and to cart away refuse and the daily cleansings from the privies in the gardens. Jefferson at first ran one road directly along the backs of each row of Pavilions. But that was hard to grade into a smooth thoroughfare, and it cut off each Pavilion from the walled garden belonging to it. Cabell made a very important suggestion, which Jefferson took up with enthusiasm.

Jefferson had first considered that all elements of the design should look toward the center, toward the Lawn. This meant that the Hotels faced the backs of the Pavilions. Cabell thought these Hotels should be turned around (along with the student dormitories linking them) to face outward, gateways welcoming the visitor, not fortresses turning their back on them. Jefferson saw that this would allow him to run his road along the outside line of the Hotels, and send spurs off of it toward the Pavilions. These spurs, passing between the walls of the private gardens, are the driveways that professors now use to take their cars to the back area of their Pavilions (FIGURE 3, p. 11).

This was a major improvement in the first design, and Jefferson gave Cabell the proper credit for it:

> The first aspect of the proposition presented to me a
> difficulty which I then thought insuperable: to wit,
> that of the approach of carriages, wood carts, etc. to the
> back of the buildings. Mr. Cabell's desire, however,
> appeared so strong, and the object of it so proper that,
> after separation [of the board members], I undertook to
> examine and try whether it could not be accomplished,

and was happy to find it practicable, by a change which was approved by General Cocke and since by Mr. Cabell, who has been lately with me. I think it a real improvement, and the greater as by throwing the Hotels and additional dormitories on a back street, it forms in fact the commencement of a regular town capable of being enlarged to any extent which future circumstances may call for. (G 4.4)

Though Jefferson was open to helpful suggestions like that made by Cabell—or like those he solicited from Thornton and Latrobe—he had the artist's ruthlessness when ideas were offered that went against his own vision for the place. John Cocke, with his experience of running an academy, was able to persuade several members of the board that the six separate Hotels would not be able to provide the kinds of services Jefferson was expecting of them. (G 3.4) He wanted to combine the Hotels into fewer and larger structures that would incorporate the student dormitories on the Ranges—thus leaving more space for the gardens, among other things. To Jefferson this was a way of returning to the old firetraps full of noise and cooking smells that he condemned in other colleges. Moreover, it broke up the intricate relationships he had worked out for all the buildings in his scheme. He reacted to this threat with the singlemindedness of his assault on the effort to move William and Mary. Declaring the board incompetent to make such a change, he resorted to "strict construction" of the Assembly plan for the university (which he himself had written at Rockfish Gap):

Separation of the students in different and unconnected rooms, by twos and twos, seems a fundamental of the plan. It was adopted by the first visitors of the Central College, stated by them in their original report to the governor as their patron, and by him laid before the legislature. It was approved and reported by the Commissioners of Rockfish Gap to the legislature. Of their opinion, indeed, we have no other evidence than their acting on it without directing a change [on that point]. (G 4.3)

Jefferson would never have let his own words stand in the way of changes *he* wanted. But he would not let the board destroy the nicely articulated scale of building-to-building throughout his architectural ensemble. As at Monticello, order was supposed to relax its hold gradually, before fading into the unstructured surrounding world.

We can now be grateful that he prevailed, if only by a somewhat autocratic move hidden beneath a legalism. The patterns created on the flanks of the original ridge are beautifully divided by the garden walls. The interplay of these outer elements with the land is a perfect complement to the broader outlines of the Lawn. A subtle counterpoint is provided by the fact that the Lawn's terraces slope down toward the south while the line of the Ranges slopes up (FIGURE 2, p. 10). One does not notice this on a first or casual visit to the place. But as one walks around the place on repeated encounters, the large lines of the overall plan are constantly being tested against the little divergences, the skipped beat, the swerve-and-recover maneuvers, that go into details of the place. As with any great work of art, one acquires by study a deeper awareness of the work's inner relationships. It is like hearing a great actor deliver Shakespeare's blank verse. The steady meter is always there, but the trained voice plays against it, delays its beat, softens or hardens the ictus on each syllable. After the regular metric run of Hamlet's Latinate opening, "Absent thee from felicity awhile," the actor may give soft equal thuds to the following monosyllables, "and in this harsh world draw thy breath in pain ..."

The beauty of the university's variety is illustrated by the famous serpentine walls around the gardens. On the university's ground plan, as it was engraved for Jefferson by Peter Maverick, these look uniform and repetitive. But in fact the walls must span dips and rises in the ground, which means they are of constantly varying height (FIGURE 3, p. 11). Above most people's eye level, they sink in places to allow differing degrees of vision into the gardens. They create a semi-privacy which does not interrupt the continuity of the whole endeavor. That they are also meant to be didactic was noticed earlier. They illustrate the principle that a wall only one brick thick will stand if (and only if) you curve it. The principle is easily illustrated. Take a piece of paper and stand it on end. It slides down. Put a sharp crease in it and the resulting two parts will buttress each other when you put it on end. Unfortunately, in the real world, single brick walls, even curving ones, respond to heat and cold over time by a swelling and shrinking of their mortar. The walls have therefore needed frequent repair—a price gladly paid to enjoy their aesthetic effect.

Going up between the wavy walls through a gap in the Lawn dormitories and out onto the Lawn is one of the best ways to experience the university. Obviously, Jefferson meant for the first orienting view to be up the three tiers of the Lawn from the south, with the Rotunda standing high in the north. But if you walk uphill from the Hotels, through the gardens, you see from your rising ground the high (three-story) backs of the Pavilions. Then, as you go up the stairs at the gap, you are climbing the height of the basement beside you. Emerging on the Lawn, you see that the Pavilions on either side of you have shrunk, to their two-story facades on the Lawn. But by the degree to which they shrink, the tall Rotunda soars, presiding over all the classical porticos, pediments, and columns around you. The Hotels have performed their propylaia function, and the gardens served as a forecourt before you reached the acropolis of the Lawn. It is a carefully orchestrated effect, and none of the changes made to the buildings over the course of 177 years has been able to destroy it.

For some, no doubt, familiarity may deaden them to the artistic accomplishment displayed here—but only as some listen to a symphony without any sense of its structure, of its departures from the norm, of the way creativity is being born out of tradition, because of tradition and not in spite of it. But the great work is always there, ready for fresh ears to hear or eyes to see.

CHAPTER FOUR

Latrobe

During the War of 1812, British troops reached the federal city and burnt the White House and the Capitol. The latter contained the congressional library. This loss, in 1814, corresponded with the need of Jefferson to ease somewhat his vertiginously accumulating debts. Though he had long desired to leave his valuable collection to an institution in "my country" (Virginia), his and the nation's needs so coalesced in 1815 that he felt obliged to sell his library to the federal government. He even sold his architectural books—several editions of Palladio, and an edition of the only architectural treatise to survive from antiquity, the *Ten Books on Architecture* by Vitruvius (Marcus Vitruvius Pollio). His surrender of these books shows that a mere two years before he began serious planning for the university he had no suspicion he would be designing classical buildings on the scale that began to dawn on him only in 1817.

When he did start thinking of such a project, he wrote Madison with great urgency: "We are sadly at a loss for a Palladio. I had three different editions, but they are at Washington, and nobody in this part of the country has one unless you have. If you have, you will greatly aid us by letting us have the use of it for a year to come." (Nov. 15, 1817) Luckily, Madison had it, and sent it.

Given this lack of the books he had always relied on in forming his designs, it is no wonder Jefferson turned to architect friends for assistance in the intimidating task of coming up with seventeen buildings of individual character. He described the project to two men, William Thornton and Benjamin Latrobe—and asked for their suggestions. He could let neither man know he was consulting the other, since they were ferocious enemies. Thornton was the amateur polymath who had improbably won the competition for designing the federal city's Capitol. Latrobe, who was given the task of raising the actual structure from Thornton's drawings, was quick to point out the unprofessional blunders in Thornton's design. Thornton, thin-skinned and self-important, responded with a series of scurrilous public attacks, including comic verses about "Benny" Latrobe, claiming that he was a foreigner traveling under a false name to escape women he had seduced. Latrobe ignored these as long as he could, and then silenced Thornton only by filing and winning a suit against him.

Jefferson was naturally diffident about imposing on the time and skills of men he, in different measure, respected and counted his friends. To Latrobe he wrote: "A few sketches, such as shall take you not more than a minute apiece, mere expressions of a first trait of the imagination, will greatly oblige us." (June 12, 1817) Despite his tactfully modest request, he must have known that both men would do whatever they could to oblige a person so important to their own history and the nation's. They responded beyond the call of courtesy. Thornton quickly (on May 27, 1817) sent a pompous dissertation on education, describing the games students should be allowed to play and where they should swim. He described the material of which bricks and mortar should be composed, and how to make columns. He also, most usefully, enclosed two actual elevations for buildings, one of which Jefferson adapted for the first building, Pavilion VII (FIGURE 4, p. 12).

Latrobe went even further, though he could be excused had he felt any hesitation about collaborating with Jefferson. Their work together on the federal buildings had not been without its tensions. Jefferson had fixed notions that Latrobe, fresh from a Europe quite different from the one Jefferson had visited in the eighteenth century, considered too conservative and too ignorant of structural principles. But their creative disagreements had led to spectacular results in the House of Representatives and Supreme Court chambers of the Capitol. Jefferson knew that Latrobe was the best architect on the continent, and Latrobe had never lost respect for his elder, however he mocked him to friends. (To an associate who lost a bid to redecorate the House chamber for an impeachment trial in 1805, Latrobe wrote: "You and I are both blockheads. Presidents [Jefferson] and Vice Presidents [Aaron Burr] are the only architects, and poets for aught I know, in the United States. Therefore let us fall down and worship them.")

It was only after he had received Thornton's moderately useful letter that Jefferson decided he must impose on the more formidable Latrobe, who was still busy as the supervising architect of the Capitol in Washington. Latrobe responded with a preliminary letter dated June 28, 1817. It contains a sketch of the university ground plan (still in Jefferson's first square design) with a hastily penned elevation of the north end, suggesting a central domed building that resembles Palladio's Villa Rotonda, flanked by Pavilions with colossal orders whose columns stand outside the colonnade—ideas Jefferson accepted. Latrobe followed up his first response with a letter written four days later:

> I have found so much pleasure in studying the plan of your college that the drawings have grown into a larger bulk than can conveniently be sent by the mail. I have put the whole upon one very large sheet, which I am very unwilling to double.

Latrobe was suggesting Jefferson might have to arrange for a special courier to carry the "very large" sheet in a crate. Jefferson was in too great need to wait for that mode of transport to be found. He asked Latrobe to use the mail:

> I am anxious to receive your draft as soon as possible ... I think your drawings had better come in the form of a roll by the mail, [or] any necessary doubling of the paper may be easily obliterated by the screw press which I possess. (July 16, 1817)

Jefferson was further tantalized by a letter of August 12 promising "a plan of the principal range of buildings ... and seven or eight elevations of Pavilions, with a general elevation of the long ranges of Pavilions and portico." There ensued a long excruciating wait for the package to arrive. Almost two months went by. Jefferson could not have known that Latrobe was going through a painful period in this interval. His son died during it, he was quarreling with President Monroe, and—to add annoyance to tragedy—a storm had forced water down his chimney, splashing soot over his papers. He tried to clean the large sheet of drawings, as he told Jefferson (Oct. 6, 1817), but only smeared it in the process. He had to do it all over again, "everything but the outline" (that is, the "plan of the principal range of buildings," those on the Lawn). Jefferson finally did receive the large sheet in October, but it has since disappeared, along with the plan of "the principal range."

Jefferson expressed his gratitude for "the beautiful drawings," since two more Pavilions would be raised in the spring building season "and we shall certainly select their fronts from these [drawings on the sheet]." (Oct. 12, 1817) When the building season did arrive, Jefferson wrote:

> We shall within [days] commence your Palladian Corinthian [Pavilion], being the left hand figure of the upper row on your paper ... [and] a third or fourth Pavilion, which would probably be your third and fifth, or perhaps second in the same line. (May 19, 1818)

Latrobe had used the mail, and since Jefferson does not mention a successful pressing of any folds, it must have been sent in a large cylinder of leather luggage. We know from the letter that the "large sheet" had an "upper row" (and therefore at least one more row), and that this top row contained at least five elevations. What was on the second row? Another five? Had Latrobe made suggestions for all ten planned professors' quarters? Two months earlier, he had promised "seven or eight" Pavilions (the uncertainty suggesting that he was still adding elevations). In the redrawing of the set, he might have gone the slight step further of drafting a complete ensemble. If he sent only eight designs, the top row would presumably have held only four of them, not five.

Or Latrobe could have filled out the second row, or made a third row, with his own drawing for the Rotunda. That a *numbered* drawing of the Rotunda, one with a relationship to other drawings, was on the sheet appears from the fact that Jefferson's own elevation for the Rotunda has on its top right corner, in Jefferson's hand, "Latrobe No. [illegible]." This is carefully crossed out, but in a different ink that allows what was written to be partially deciphered. And Jefferson's floor plan for the library in the Rotunda (the dome room) has this: "[Latrobe's] Rotunda, reduced to the proportions of the Pantheon." Here the first word is erased, making it read simply "Rotunda, reduced to the proportions ..." This is not the only time Latrobe's name was erased from a drawing. The same thing happened to a mention of Latrobe on the drawing for Pavilion IX—though on that sheet a second mention was allowed to stand.

Joseph Lasala, in his thorough study of all Jefferson's drawings for the university, says that Jefferson "tried to conceal
Latrobe's connection with the Rotunda."[1] One might even
think that the loss of such an important large roll, by a man
who saved everything as meticulously as Jefferson always did,
could be "destruction of the evidence" for his reliance on
Latrobe. But anyone could have crossed out or erased the name
in these three cases (it is, after all, a different ink that was used
for the crossing out). Some misguided admirer of Jefferson
might later have tried to preserve his reputation for originality
by crossing out or erasing Latrobe's name And the roll might
have been cut up by Jefferson, for easier use of individual elevations in making his own drawings or in explaining particular
points to his master contractor or master workmen, or they
might have handled the intact sheet in ways that damaged it.
Jefferson had to commit drawings to his workmen on the site
when he was up at Monticello, or (once or twice a year) when
he went to Bedford County to supervise his other plantation at
Poplar Forest.

In any case, Jefferson seems to have been quite open in
wanting and acknowledging Latrobe's help, and it has always
been clear that Latrobe played a great part in the designs for the
Lawn. How great it is hard to establish because of the missing
"large sheet." But in 1920, Philip Alexander Bruce wrote, in
what is still the best general history of the university:

> The influence of Latrobe is distinctly reflected in
> Pavilions III and V, and it possibly comes out also in
> several of the Pavilions erected after the incorporation

of the university [in 1819] but this cannot be posi-
tively stated owing to the loss of the drawings. It is
most strongly suspected in Pavilion X, which closely
follows III; and also in Pavilion VIII.[2]

Bruce names Pavilions III and V because III and V were the
next ones built after Jefferson said he was using Latrobe's
designs for them, making "your Corinthian Palladian" the
design for III (FIGURE 11, p. 54). Bruce names Pavilion IX
(FIGURE 7, p. 15) because of the one surviving mention of
Latrobe on the drawing. Pavilion X he seems to mention
because it is so different, as built, from its own drawing (which
has only two side windows instead of four).

Bruce seemed to have exhausted all that could be said about
Latrobe's role in 1920. But then an art historian at the university,
Malcolm Bell, began to do some fancy detective work. Since he is
an archaeologist who has worked on Greek temples in Sicily,
where his knowledge of mathematical proportions for the classical
orders was brought constantly into play, he was struck by the fact
that the middle gap between Pavilion V's columns (the intercolumniation) was wider than the other (four) intercolumniations
(FIGURE 6, p. 14). This suggested to him a Vitruvian formula,
and the columns seemed to be the right height for that formula.
When he checked Jefferson's drawing for the Pavilion, he saw that
all the intercolumniations were drawn as uniform. Somebody was
sneaking Vitruvius onto the Lawn. Who could it be?

Jefferson had owned an edition of Vitruvius, but he sold it
to the Library of Congress, where it was in the very building for
which Latrobe was the attending architect in 1817. It is true

that Jefferson knew some Vitruvian formulae from Palladio's use of the ancient treatise, but Jefferson did not seem to be especially interested in the Vitruvian aspects of his favorite theorist. He showed more concern for the historical exemplars in famous Roman buildings, reproducing their entablatures (the horizontal area running across the top of the columns, articulated into cornice, frieze, architrave, and other minor elements). It was not very surprising then for Joseph Lasala, working carefully with the measurements of Jefferson's drawings, to write that "there is not a single example of the ideal [Vitruvian] eustyle intercolumniation on any of the Jeffersonian buildings at the University of Virginia."[3] Yet a eustyle pattern is precisely what Bell's classically trained eye was picking out on Pavilion V.

What does eustyle mean? Literally, it is Greek for "fine-columned"—*eu*- being the same prefix we know in words like euphemism (fine-speaking), eugenics (fine-breeding), eulogy (fine-account), and so on. Vitruvius contrasted the eustyle with four other forms of intercolumniation—araeostyle (widest-columned, exemplified on the Lawn in Pavilion I), diastyle (wide-columned), systyle (close-columned, exemplified in the Rotunda), pycnostyle (closest-columned, exemplified in Pavilion X). All these orders can have a uniform space between all their columns. But Vitruvius preferred the eustyle, where the central space must be wider than the flanking ones, "opening a cleared entry." (Vitruvius 3.3.6) Vitruvius thought the order had been invented by his Hellenistic hero, Hermogenes. This is what he called "fine."

Any spacing of columns is considered legitimate in classical art only if all the other parts are in correct mathematical relationships with it—height of base, height and width of column, and height and style of the entablature's many components. These measurements make up the basic grammar of classical architecture, and show why Jefferson, to express his contempt for the architects of the Virginia colony, said that not one of them could draw a correct order. The unit of measurement for all these parts is the module, which Vitruvius equates with the width of the column at its base. The standard gap between columns was, for the eustyle, two and a quarter times the width of the column (1:2¼), but for the central gap three times its width (1:3). Then the proper height for the columns would be nine times the module (1:9), according to the edition of Vitruvius that Jefferson had owned.

That looked about right to Bell, judging the height of Pavilion V's columns by eye. But when he measured the columns precisely, he found that they are three inches short of nine modules. Was Lasala correct, then, in saying there are no eustyle orders on the Lawn? This is where Bell's detective instincts came into play. He noted that three inches is exactly the height of one course of bricks, with their mortar. He found that Jefferson had specified nine modules for this building, but the bricklayers had raised the walls only to the height of the next-over Pavilion (III).

It is significant that all three Pavilions with a wider central intercolumniation are ones that had already been attributed to Latrobe (V, VIII, X). It is as if Latrobe, who was not mainly a classicist in his own work, were paying a tribute to his old friend by intensive application of Vitruvius to the project he had proposed. In working on Pavilion X, Bell had to consider

FIGURE 16. *West facade of Pavilion* X

a watercolor drawing of it that is not in Jefferson's plain-line style (FIGURE 16). For a time it was attributed to Jefferson's granddaughter, Cornelia Randolph, who did make watercolors of Monticello and other buildings. But she would have worked from the finished building, and would therefore not have omitted the balcony and the two outer bays of windows on the building as completed. The drawing has more recently been attributed to Jefferson's master builder, John Neilson, from whose large collection of drawings it has come down to us. But it is not on any kind of paper Neilson used for his own drawings. Why would he have made such an elegant drawing before the Pavilion was built, or have omitted the balcony and side windows if he drew the piece after it was built?

FIGURE 17. *Elevation of Rotunda, flanked by end Pavilions IX and X*

Bell noticed that the style and materials of the drawing—done in India ink, watercolor, and white ink, and with an inked frame—are those of Latrobe, who gave his presentation drawings a three-dimensional feel by adding cast shadows to the architectural details. Latrobe had said that what he prepared for Jefferson had "a larger bulk" than the mail could handle. Bell is suggesting that other drawings were rolled up with the missing great sheet and the missing plan of the Lawn—including this drawing for what became Pavilion X. Jefferson altered the design in several ways to produce the actual building.

Bell sees Latrobe's hand in another picture, done in the same style as that of Pavilion X, this one using pencil, pen, and watercolor, with touches of gouache. It is the elevation of the Rotunda and Pavilions IX and X (FIGURE 17). This, too, has been attributed to Neilson, but it has other characteristics of Latrobe's presentation drawings, the sketchy clouds in the sky and vegetation on the ground. And it, again, lacks certain details in the finished buildings. The same questions have to be asked about it that were just asked about the drawing of Pavilion X. Why would Neilson have made such a formal drawing before the buildings were completed? But if he made the drawing after their completion, he would have reproduced the buildings more accurately. Nor would he have drawn the Lawn without its terraces, as if the Rotunda and the Pavilions stood on the same flat surface. These features are easily explained if the drawing is by Latrobe, who never saw the site.

If Bell is right, then, Latrobe deserves more credit than he has been given for the Rotunda—and the crossed-out and erased references to him on Jefferson's Rotunda drawings are confirmed in their obvious meaning: "Latrobe's Rotunda ..." Some may think that it detracts from Jefferson's creativity for him to have collaborated so closely with Latrobe. But the overall design of the university, the working out of its details, the conception of an ensemble and the scaling of all its parts, the continual adjustments made in the course of its realization—all these are Jefferson's, as is the responsibility for choosing among Latrobe's designs, assigning them their place on the Lawn, individuating each Pavilion, negotiating its relationship with the terrace and colonnade in front, with the variously precipitous plunges of the ground behind.

Jefferson was always known to have chosen models for his buildings from the drawings of men he admired—as when he adapted Palladio's Villa Rotonda when submitting a proposal for the president's home in Washington. How is that different from adapting Latrobe's drawings? Latrobe, after all, is considered by some (I am one) to be America's greatest architect. It is a mark of honor for the university to have had him so intimately connected with its buildings. Jefferson had accepted the ideas of a far inferior artist when he patterned Pavilion VII after Thornton's drawing. It should also be remembered that Jefferson was severely pressed for time in putting up the university while carrying on all his other activities as the manager of two working plantations, an adviser to political allies, and a correspondent with philosophes around the world. In 1819, when disagreement over the western Range and Hotels made Jefferson shift his attention, ahead of time, to the eastern Pavilions, it turned out that he had not yet designed a single one. Since he had a rich store of Latrobe's ideas at hand, he must have felt that he could easily pick from among them when he had to make final decisions on what to put where. And, sure enough, when the time came, he was able to complete the drawings for all five Pavilions on the east Lawn within three weeks.

We do not know, of course, that all the remaining Pavilions, after the one Thornton inspired, were adapted from Latrobe, but at least half of those on the Lawn—and perhaps more—seem to have been. Yet that did not relieve Jefferson of the necessity for making adaptations of the models provided him. In at least one case, perhaps more, Latrobe had drawn a structure that did not fit the assigned width called for on the Lawn. And it was probably Jefferson who chose the historical Roman exemplar for entablatures on each Pavilion—that was the kind of scholarship that Latrobe had little taste for and that Jefferson loved. These entablatures were to be occasions for the classical lectures that he envisioned, the kind that made him clear duties for his teaching instruments when the Italian capitals arrived from Italy.

The more serious way Jefferson could take Latrobe's ideas and enrich them is seen in the interior of the Rotunda. Latrobe had suggested "below, a couple or four rooms for janitors or tutors;

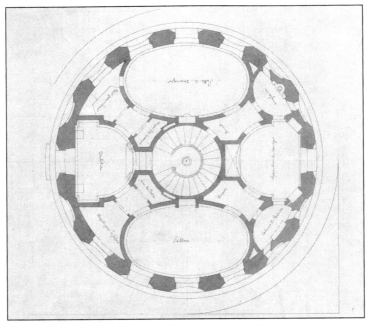

FIGURE 18. *Plan for the ground floor of the Désert de Retz*

above, a room for chemical or other lectures; above, a circular
lecture room under the dome." (July 24, 1817) Jefferson articulates
the interior of the Rotunda with great elegance. At the basement
level he put space for chemical experiments and for a natural history museum, to which he donated the first specimens from his
collection. On the entry level, he imitated a feature from a home
he fondly remembered visiting in France, the circular Désert de
Retz built in the form of a huge ruined column. That building
had two oval rooms on its first floor, disposed on either side of a
central winding staircase (FIGURE 18). Jefferson put two large

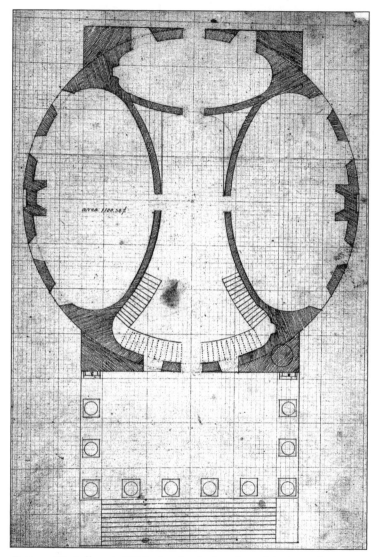

area 1100 sq.f

FIGURE 19. *Jefferson's 1823 plan for the first floor of the Rotunda*

FIGURE 20. *The Rotunda's interior stairs*

oval rooms on either side of his great door, and a third oval room at the far end from it. This left an hourglass-shaped hallway of lines that curve beautifully around the exterior of the three oval rooms (FIGURE 19). This has been called the first cyma (double-curve) shape used in American architecture. Latrobe would have loved it if he could have seen it, since it suggests the lines curved within curves of Sir John Soane's work, a man Latrobe had admired in England.

The crowning touch is the use of the curved spaces Jefferson makes in his two flights of interior stairs framing the entrance. Each begins by bending one way, around the outer wall of one of the oval rooms, and then switches at the landing level to bend

FIGURE 21. *The Rotunda's dome room*

in the opposite direction to hug the exterior wall of the round
structure (FIGURE 20). The genius of this building, which has the
shape of a circle in a cylinder, could not be more expressively
completed. Jefferson was known for his dislike of the grand stairways in the central hall of plantation great houses. In his designs
for his own two homes and for those of friends, he hid tiny stairs,
little better than ladders, in inconspicuous spots. But where a
grand staircase was appropriate, he created a stunning and original one.

On the top floor, under the dome, where Latrobe wanted a
"circular lecture room," Jefferson put his library. Any of the
obvious ways of lining up bookshelves, in rectangular configurations, would have been in conflict with the circular walls and
concave ceiling. Jefferson, instead, put them on radial lines
emanating from the empty center of the room. These radiating

rows of books are covered at their end nearest the center space by double columns holding up the balcony (FIGURE 21). If one stands at the exact center of the room, one cannot even tell that there are books behind the sets of paired columns. The combination of beauty and practicality shows Jefferson at his very best. None of this was in Latrobe's mind.

We can see the Rotunda's magnificent interior as Jefferson designed it because of the fine restoration of it in the 1970s. That restoration was needed because the Rotunda was gutted by fire in 1895 and rebuilt with a different interior in 1896-1898. The fire started in the Annex to the Rotunda that had been built by Jefferson's old pupil, Robert Mills, in 1851-1853. This long Annex stretched from the north side of the Rotunda, leaving the facade facing the Lawn untouched; but it put an imposingly pedimented portico on the north end of the complex, reorienting the whole. Mills created a new grand entrance on the side away from the Lawn. When the fire was discovered in the Annex, professors tried to dynamite the connecting link with the Rotunda; but Mills had built too well—the dynamite could not bring that section down, and the fire spread to the Rotunda. Students hurried books down the stairs, or threw them out of windows into blankets held as nets by their fellows below— about a third of the books were saved. Firefighting equipment called for by telegraph from Richmond, Lynchburg, and Staunton was raced on trains toward Charlottesville; but it could not arrive in time to save the Rotunda. Townspeople helped university personnel in wetting down Pavilions I and II to keep sparks from igniting them—and dynamite *did* work on the terraces connecting the Pavilions to the Rotunda.

As soon as the fire was over, the first battle of restoration began. A local architect quickly assured the board that there was little recoverable from the destruction but part of the brick shell. The board turned to the most prestigious architectural firm then in operation, McKim, Mead, and White. The senior partner in the firm, Charles McKim, was in that very year building a spectacular rotunda-style library for Columbia University. But another partner, Stanford White, was available to work in Charlottesville. White is still famous for the tabloid death he would meet in 1906 at the hands of an enraged husband. But while the University of Virginia had his attention in the 1890s, they asked him, besides rebuilding the Rotunda, to design three new buildings to seal off the end of the Lawn. They turned to him again in the new century (1906) to create a home for the first president of the university, Carr's Hill— it was one of the last designs he completed.

White had misgivings about closing off the Lawn, but the board assured him that was its desire. White sank the buildings to one-story facades on an added and lower tier of the Lawn, with multistory back elevations, like those of the Pavilions themselves. The central building was named Cabell Hall and one of the flanking ones Cocke Hall, for Jefferson's principal coadjutors in the university project. The other flanking building should have been called, for the next most important founder of the school (and its second rector), Madison Hall. Instead, it is named Rouss Hall, for the rich alumnus who put up the money for it. (A Madison Hall was built, off the Lawn, in 1907.)

The battle over restoring the Rotunda pitted the faculty against the board, and the board won. Faculty members wanted to restore Jefferson's interior exactly. The board, which had wrestled for some years with the fact that the library now exceeded its housing, wanted more space for books. Stanford White wanted an opportunity to create something new, something to compete with his partner-rival's work for Columbia's library. He said that eliminating Jefferson's floor with the oval rooms would allow him to treat the whole interior (except the basement) as one space, a space devoted entirely to books. He claimed that this was closer to Jefferson's design than what he was forced to build. Jefferson needed class and meeting space because the first-floor classrooms of the Pavilions could not hold larger assemblies. By 1895, White argued, the university had other auditoriums, so Jefferson's first preference could at last be realized, giving the whole building over to its library.

The myth that White's interior was proto-Jeffersonian would live for decades and be enshrined in Bruce's great five-volume history of the university. The increased shelving on balconies was made possible by White's running huge Corinthian columns straight from the entrance level up to the dome (FIGURE 22). In this configuration, the building was able to hold the university library from 1898 to 1939, when Jefferson's Anatomical Theater was torn down to make room for the Alderman Library. (Today that building, though it had been much altered by 1939, would never be destroyed.) Eventually, White's vision for the Rotunda was so accepted as Jeffersonian that the president of the university was surprised when the school's professor of architectural history, Frederick Nichols, told him that it was not in fact what Jefferson had built. That was in the 1950s, when the neglected career of Jefferson as architect was being rediscovered, and it began the

FIGURE 22. *The Rotunda interior as designed by Stanford White*

second battle of restoration, since Nichols wanted to clear out the White interior and return to Jefferson's design. But by the fifties some preservationists, criticizing the "rebuilding" of much of Colonial Williamsburg, condemned the substitution of replicas for real artifacts, however partial or altered. Why, by their argument, remove the old, a genuine Stanford White, for the new, an imitation Thomas Jefferson?

That attitude was growing as Nichols waged his rearguard battle for a return to Jefferson's dome room. He finally won that battle when White's work was torn down in 1973; but if the battle had been prolonged much beyond that point, the advocates of White would very likely have prevailed, since the codes of preservation are now so much stricter.[4] Certain people at the university still regret the disappearance of White's work. One told me that White was truer to Jefferson's model and inspiration, the Pantheon in Rome, since that has only one huge interior space. But the vertical space in White's Rotunda was not shaped like the wider room in the Pantheon. White's interior walls are, as in Rome, the same height as the dome; but the inner space is experienced within the central ring of columns, which the Pantheon does not have, so it is more vertical and cylindrical than circular. Jefferson's dome room above the first floor was actually more like the mushroom crown of the Pantheon's interior, as Jefferson noted on his drawing for the dome room: "[Latrobe's] Rotunda reduced to the proportions of the Pantheon." His dome room has walls only roughly a third the height of the dome, but the dome is "brought down" in feeling because the inner circle of columns reduces the width of perceived space. It was a brilliant solution to the problem of having a room that was like the Pantheon, but which could not be one open space within, given the need to find room for books. The ring of columns with radiating shelves provided that.

Some people do not realize that only the top part of the Rotunda's interior is shaped like the Pantheon's. In part this is because it is so commonly said that the Rotunda is a half-sized version of the Pantheon. Anyone who goes directly from experiencing the vast concavity in Rome to a sight of the library in Charlottesville must find it laughable that two Rotundas could equal in space one Pantheon. What Jefferson said is that he made the building half of the Pantheon's *diameter.* But that reduces the space to a quarter, a principle most easily explained with a square figure.

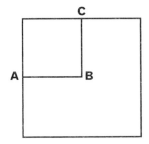

If *a* to *b* is half the diameter, so is *b* to *c*—Jefferson rightly explained the result on the back of his drawing of the dome room: "The diameter of the building, 77 feet, being one half that of the Pantheon, consequently one fourth its area, and one eighth its volume."

Others objected to the restoration of Jefferson's Rotunda because the result is not an exact replica. Numerical relationships mattered to Jefferson, and the university's professor of architectural preservation, Mario di Valmarana, told me that modern fire codes made it impossible to give the risers on Jefferson's great stairways the exact height he had prescribed. (Valmarana should know about preservation—his family still owns and maintains Palladio's Villa Rotonda in the Veneto.) Other features were required by safety ordinances or insurance exigencies—a new railing around the library's intermediate balcony, for instance. Modern materials, cheaper and stronger, were substituted for some of Jefferson's original components—in some cases because the new interior had to be fireproofed. Aluminum filters were used on the dome for acoustic control. Space had to be found for modern amenities like heating and air-conditioning units and conduits. Costs were cut by casting in plaster the forty Corinthian capitals on the library's columns instead of carving them from black locust and painting them white, as Jefferson had. All these things said in objection are true. But even at Monticello, where the staff not only tries to use original materials but to work them with original eighteenth-century tools, modern features have to be inconspicuously inserted. The upkeep of a remaining fabric, that is, requires constant renovation, which at times means modernization.

Despite all the good arguments for retaining the White version of the Rotunda (and they are good arguments), I am glad that the case for rebuilding Jefferson's interior won out. The principal authentic work on this site is the original complex of seventeen buildings. They should be seen as a whole, each part interpreting the other parts. White's intrusion of an alien design impeded this larger effort of preservation. In the Rotunda itself, the play of spatial volumes, the curving responses of room to room, the monumental stairways, the radiating book shelves, the travel of light from the oculus around the dome room—all these things must be seen in tactile and three-dimensional form if we are to appreciate what Jefferson accomplished in this supreme work. The drawings are no substitute. *They* are authentic, but they cry for completion in the space Jefferson reserved for them. I have seen the dome room when it is filled for a banquet. I have seen it when it is semideserted and students seek it out as a quiet place to read or write in. If I lived in Charlottesville, I would go there to write myself. It is an inspired and inspiring place.

CHAPTER FIVE

"Universal Confessors" Arrive

By the beginning of 1825, seven and a half years after the cornerstone was laid for Central College, the University of Virginia was ready to begin its first term of instruction. The faculty roster was not entirely filled, but it soon would be. Jefferson had been compelled to seek far off for his teachers, but they were all capable, and some were more than that, despite their general youth. (Five of the first six expected to be on hand at the school's opening were still in their twenties.) But then, at the last minute, the school's opening had to be delayed. As the scheduled date (February 1) approached, three of the professors coming from England were not there. They had embarked over three months earlier, and Jefferson feared that the ship carrying them had gone down. He had to run advertisements in the newspapers telling students not to come on the announced date after all, but to watch for news of the real opening, whenever that might be. To his vast relief, the three men arrived on February 10, when their slow ship, the ill-named *Competitor,* finally reached Norfolk. Much of their difficult time aboard they had been stalled in the English Channel by storms.

On their late arrival at these shores, the English professors wondered what kind of country they had reached, since the pilot who came out beyond the Capes to conduct them did not know the answer to a question that had kept them in suspense during their long trip. Inquisitive about their new land, they had debated whether "Mr. Adams or General Jackson" had won last fall's election. The pilot did not know the answer. He had the excuse that the election had been thrown into the House of Representatives and had not been resolved until the day before *Competitor* landed—but the newcomers could not know this, and they concluded too hastily that Americans were ignorant of their own affairs. They proceeded to Richmond, where Jefferson's son-in-law, who had recently been Virginia's governor, Thomas Mann Randolph, greeted them. The sharpest observer in the three, Robley Dunglison, Jefferson's first professor of medicine, noticed that Randolph was "an exceedingly well-informed gentleman, but eccentric even to aberration."[1]

He also found the speech and accents of Virginians eccentric, as when someone asked where he was going to "locate" rather than where he was going to live. He enjoyed the comment of "a kind of Mr. Malaprop" who said that "the universal confessors were arrived." But what he took as comical may have been satirical. There was a good deal of skepticism about the idea of bringing foreigners into Virginia for the instruction of Americans—and not only in Virginia. Newspapers from as far away as Philadelphia and Connecticut had taken Jefferson's action as an attack on American learning. The *Connecticut Journal* editorialized: "Mr. Jefferson might as well have said that his taverns [Hotels] and dormitories should not be built with American bricks and have sent to Europe for them." Even some of Jefferson's own board members regretted that so many professors were not American. John Cocke wrote to Cabell: "Do save us from this inundation of foreigners if it is possible."[2]

Jefferson himself was unhappy about hunting for his faculty in Europe. He had for years opposed sending Americans to study there, where they could imbibe alien values. But his first efforts to recruit a faculty in America had all been thwarted—qualified men had either turned him down or been, like Thomas Cooper, too controversial for the Virginia legislature to accept them. Facing these rejections, Jefferson as usual moralized the inevitable, concluding that Harvard and Yale should not be deprived of good teachers just to benefit Virginia—it would not be "honorable or moral to endeavor to seduce them from their stations." (Oct. 5, 1824) He had, furthermore, begun to think Harvard and Yale were "foreign" in the climate of the 1820s. As we shall see, one of his motives for pushing so hard to open a school at home was to prevent Virginians from being corrupted at northern colleges.

He knew, however, that he would face resistance to his imported learning. He tried at the outset to keep his purpose secret. When he dispatched Francis Walker Gilmer as his talent scout "to the universities of Oxford, Cambridge, and Edinburgh," (April 26, 1824) he planted a cover story in the cooperative Richmond *Enquirer,* saying that Gilmer was shopping for nothing but books and scientific apparatus on this trip. Gilmer took delight in his clandestine assignment and wrote to friends, "I shall be passing rapidly through Baltimore, and wish to be incog. ... Secrecy is all important to me in every way."[3]

Gilmer, thirty-three years old, was not Jefferson's first choice for what the university's historian, Philip Alexander Bruce, calls "the English Mission" to find teachers. As regularly happened when Jefferson needed good judgment and loyalty to the university, he turned to Joseph Cabell, asking him to go abroad during the summer recess of the Assembly. Only when Cabell informed him that his family and plantation affairs would not let him travel (C Oct. 27, 1823) did Jefferson turn to a young favorite of his. Gilmer, he believed, was "the best educated subject we [of Virginia] have raised since the Revolution." (April 26, 1824) He would have been pleased if Gilmer's bid for the hand of his favorite granddaughter, Ellen, had been successful, but Ellen had outgrown her childhood sweetheart, to Gilmer's distress.[4] When Jefferson asked Gilmer to be become his professor of law at the university, Gilmer rejected the offer, just as Ellen had rejected him. But Gilmer had never been to Europe, so he agreed to go there as Jefferson's academic head hunter.

It was a difficult assignment—he was asked to woo six men to leave their own careers, in their own countries, in order to join an untried experiment in the New World. Gilmer had to sail in the spring and search in the summer, when the universities were not in session: "At this season of the year, no man in England is where he ought to be, except perhaps those of Fleet and of Newgate [prisons]. Every little country school master, who never saw a town, is gone, as they say, to the country, that is to Scotland to shoot grouse, to Doncaster to see a race, or to Cheltenham [Springs] to dose himself with that vile water."[5] And if he did run anyone down, find his credentials good, and persuade him to accept a post, he had to require that he finish up his present business immediately and get on a ship in the fall to reach Virginia by Christmas. Yet Jefferson had chosen the right man to accomplish this mission impossible. It is a tribute to Gilmer's charming manner and focused energy that he netted five men, almost meeting his assigned quota of six.

Gilmer learned to capitalize on the particular situations of his quarry. Robley Dunglison, for instance, was a young doctor whose prospects were favored by the medical establishment of London, but who needed instant cash to marry the woman he loved. Travel money promised by Gilmer, an advance on his salary, and the prospect of student fees in Virginia tempted Dunglison. There was also the promise of free lodging in one of the new Pavilions designed by the famous Jefferson. Gilmer had taken with him large numbers of the Maverick engravings of the university's layout, and he described in lavish detail the accommodations being promised—some would feel that their future home had been misrepresented to them when they reached Virginia and discovered the still raw state of the Lawn in 1825.

When Gilmer made his offer to Dunglison, the Scot said that his response would depend on his fiancée's agreeing to cross the ocean with him. He rushed to her house, but could not immediately ask her since she was entertaining some prominent friends of her father. But as soon as he could get her aside and assure himself of her agreement, he returned to a relieved Gilmer and accepted the professorship. The marriage had to be rapidly concluded for him to reach Virginia for the opening session—but then he and his bride spent the first three and a half months of their marriage on a ship immobilized or making slow progress toward their future. They got to know the two other professors traveling with them—Thomas Key (mathematics) and George Long (Greek and Latin): "Both were dogmatical, as the students of Cambridge have often been considered to be; but Mr. Long was much the more amiable." Mr. Key "was fond of controversies, and not always courteous, so that he got into numerous personal altercations. He was, indeed, one of the most impracticable men with whom I have ever been thrown in contact." Key made life miserable for the *Competitor*'s captain, complaining and sneering. It was a nightmare honeymoon for the Dunglisons to be thrown continually into his company. It would be hard to remain a universal confessor with such a colleague.

Even on the carriage ride from Richmond to Charlottesville, Key was acting the blowhard: "Mr. Key, whose sentiments in politics were decidedly liberal if not radical, emphatically declared that this was 'the country in which he would wish to live and die,' yet in the course of a year or two he emphatically stated that 'he would rather live in England on six pence a day' than on the handsome income he received form his labors at the university." Dunglison may have been happy to get out of the carriage while they all "walked a mile to the town and stayed at the Stone Tavern."

The sight of the Lawn that greeted them on the next morning was not reassuring. The Rotunda lacked the stairs, columns, and roof of its portico. Work was going on sporadically to finish or repair the Pavilions and Hotels, many of which had already begun to leak. Some Pavilions looked rather shabby within, since master builders had been living in them while they completed their work. Subordinate workers had taken up their quarters in the student dormitories, and slave workers in the dormitory basements. (G 3.12) Workers were used to going where they wanted in this complex, with a self-important bustle and noise that annoyed the newcomers from England. The workers also used whatever privy was nearest their current job, including the single-unit "necessaries" reserved to each professor in his own garden. There were two dozen single-unit privies in and around the gardens, often abutting the serpentine walls, and two multiple-unit public privies, to the side of the Ranges. (G 7.3)

Dunglison drew as his home Pavilion X, the last one on the east Lawn, and noticed at once its lack of amenities (it had, for instance, no closets or cupboards). The giant frieze in the formal dining room seemed to him out of scale with the size of the room: "The heavy cornices in the rooms of the Palladian style were far from pleasing." Until he could buy a bed, he and his wife had to sleep on the floor. Dunglison had as yet no horse, to ride the one mile into Charlottesville for supplies; and merchants had not yet set up vending places near the university. He wanted to hire a servant to live in the basement, for cooking and washing and cleaning, but he was told that good ones were not easily found. He and others would soon buy slaves for this purpose.

There were only two professors awaiting Dunglison and his shipmates when they reached Charlottesville, men who could advise them on where to find supplies and services—Charles Bonnycastle (professor of natural philosophy) and George

Blaettermann (professor of modern languages). They, too, had been hired by Gilmer in England, but having taken a better and faster ship to America, they arrived before Christmas in 1824. These five foreigners were soon joined by two American citizens who were also foreign-born—John Patton Emmet (professor of chemistry) in Ireland, and George Tucker (professor of moral philosophy) in Bermuda. Emmet had attended and taught at West Point, and Tucker was a relative of Henry St. George Tucker, the patriot lawyer of Williamsburg.

The oldest man in the group (forty-five) would not join them on the Lawn for another year—John Tayloe Lomax. Jefferson wanted not only an American but a Virginian to be his professor of law, since he would have to teach the American system of government, for which Jefferson himself drew up the prescribed texts. But this was the hardest chair to fill—six men were offered it and turned him down. Gilmer, who had been the first to refuse the post, before he went talent searching in Britain, later reconsidered, but was prevented from accepting by the ill health that led to his early death. (He died, at thirty-six, half a year before Jefferson did.) Jefferson, on Madison's recommendation, asked Lomax to leave his law practice in Fredericksburg and move to the Lawn, where, as an American, as a Virginian, as a teacher of American law, and as the oldest professor, he was voted by the others to be chairman of the faculty. Its meetings were held in his Pavilion (III)—but he would depart in four years to become a judge.

Most faculty members got along with each other. Three of the bachelors found Virginia brides. George Long married the sister of Jefferson's master contractor, Arthur Brockenbrough, who was living temporarily in Hotel D on the east Range. And Emmet, the Irishman, married the sister of Tucker, the Bermudan. Charles Bonnycastle, hired in England by Gilmer, married a Miss Tutt of Loudoun County. The exception to marital bliss came from the despotic linguist, Blaettermann, who whipped his wife in public and was the only one of the original professors to be, eventually, fired.

Emmet chafed most at his narrow quarters and sought *Lebensraum*. He began to build onto his Pavilion almost at once, and he demanded for his classes not only the chemistry laboratory in the basement of the Rotunda, but the museum space there as well (the museum was moved upstairs into the smallest oval room). He also agreed to Jefferson's desire to supervise a botanical garden, to be placed at the south end of the Lawn. Emmet had need of space, since he managed to acquire a menagerie for the study of native animals. When his bear proved a nuisance to the neighbors, he had it cooked up for them as a banquet in Pavilion I.

The professors' problems were not with their fellows but with the students. Many of the first students were sons of plantation owners, used to be being waited on by slaves and to maintaining their own horses and guns. Jefferson had convinced himself that these young men were innately noble, "yeoman farmers," uncorrupted by cities and banks, who could be trusted with the liberty he thought their natural birthright. Not only were they allowed to choose their own program of study; they were also to be largely self-governing through their own elected "censors" (the Roman word for moral supervisors). Not all the students were from the plantation-owning class, but

those who were set the swaggering tone for others. Slave owners were used to giving, not taking, orders.

The opening spring period of the school went without
major incident. But the board, under Jefferson's prompting,
wanted to crowd as much instruction as possible into the students' time at the university, so there was no summer break.
The students were to study, without interruption, ten and a half
months a year, with time off only in the Christmas and New
Year season. The first group of students thought they had found
an ingenious way, during the long Virginia summer, to liberate
themselves at least briefly from this schedule. They capitalized
on a date Jefferson himself had made solemn, and petitioned
the faculty to be let off for ten days to celebrate the Fourth of
July. Dunglison, who was secretary of the faculty, directed the
students' petition up the mountain to the rector. But Jefferson
became again the strict constructionist, saying he had no
authority to change a provision that had behind it the authority
of the state Assembly:

> By the act of the legislature establishing the university,
> its government is committed to a Board of Visitors
> with authority to establish rules for that purpose.
> Among the rules established by them is that which
> declares there shall be one vacation only in the year,
> and that that shall be from the fifteenth of December
> to the last day of January. This statute can be repealed
> or suspended by the Board of Visitors only, and conse-
> quently it is not in my power, a single member of that
> board, to authorize a dispensation with it. Its object

was to avoid the common abuse by which two or three months of the year are lost to the students under the name of vacations. The thread of their studies is broken, and more time still to be expended in recovering it. This loss at their ages, from sixteen and upwards, is irreparable to them. Time will not suspend its flow during these intermissions of study. The regulation was established by the Visitors with a single eye to the good of the students; and my confidence in the discretion of those [students] of the university, grounded on the correctness of their conduct hitherto, is too firmly fixed to doubt of their willing acquiescence in what has been done for them alone. Repeating therefore my incompetence to the dispensation proposed, with assurances that the part I take in the affairs of the university is with the sole view of rendering them worthy in themselves, valuable members of society, and fit successors of their fathers in the government of their country [Virginia], I pray you to accept for the faculty and yourself [the secretary who had addressed him] the tender of my great esteem and respect. (June 29, 1825)

All very reasonable, all very confident that rational young will show a "willing acquiescence in what has been done for them alone." But it was a confidence misplaced. As summer turned to autumn, the nativist streak in the students came out. They began to mock and defy the "foreign" faculty, especially what Dunglison had called the "dogmatical" Cantabrigians, Key and Long. They shouted insults outside their Pavilions, and threw stones through Long's window. Jefferson, on first report of this, dismissed it as boyish pranks, but his daughter Martha knew better—she said the ruffians were led by a "rich fool" (of the plantation class).[6] Dunglison, who had become a friend of Martha by this point, agreed with her: "The first regulations of the university, which were mainly I believe his [Jefferson's] work, were the results of his reflections, but did not act well, and had to be abandoned—some of them, I know, with great reluctance on his part."

Things came quickly to a head. Key and Long, terrorized by masked students, refused to work under such conditions and submitted their resignations in September. The board refused to accept them, saying the two men were bound by their five-year contract; but the October 7 meeting of the board, scheduled beforehand for one morning, took five days of confrontation with the students, at which Jefferson became too emotional to continue speaking. He was especially stunned by the fact that one of the three ring leaders, whom the board was expelling, was his own great-nephew, son of Thomas Mann Randolph's sister— and Jefferson was in searing conflict with Thomas Mann, his son-in-law, at just this time. Yet he dutifully gave way to the board's stricter new rules, admitting that "loose principle in the ethics of schoolboy combination" could not be indulged.

The Hotel system soon proved just as unworkable as self-government by the students. Jefferson had hoped that the people managing the Hotels would compete to provide the best food and services for the students. Instead, they lured the boys with alcohol and gambling. In January of the new year (1826), the first student who would become famous enrolled, Edgar Allan

Poe. He was there in time to record the opening of the library in the Rotunda, and to make good use of it. But he also ran up a string of gambling debts at the Hotels that made his guardian remove him from the school after one year. (Jefferson died in the middle of his year there, and there is no evidence that they met.) The civil authorities had also to be called in to prosecute neighborhood taverns that were serving the students liquor.

The problems of student discipline could not be solved with one meeting, and they came up again at the spring session of the board. A majority on the board thought that the school required a more vigorous form of government. They advocated appointing a full-time president (as opposed to being ruled by the intermittent meetings of the board and the continuing but distant attention of its rector). Jefferson, opposed in principle to energetic government, argued that the rector and the faculty chairman could, between them, handle any situation. The board deferred at first to its esteemed leader, but then tried to change his mind by saying the university could not solve its problem of finding a Virginian to teach law unless it sweetened an offer to William Wirt, the famous lawyer and writer, by making the presidency an adjunct to that chair. Jefferson was still opposed (it did not help that Wirt had written an adoring biography of Patrick Henry, a man Jefferson considered a shallow demagogue). The board was able to override Jefferson on this, but Wirt turned it down. The best the board could come up with was an increase in the authority of the proctor, making poor Arthur Brockenbrough move from being the university's chief contractor to being its head of police. For decades to come, any attempt to create the post of president would be shot down by quoting Jefferson's memo against the idea. It was not till 1904 that a president was appointed.

Problems of discipline continued after Jefferson's death. Things would get worse before they got better in the early history of the school. The South's was a culture of violence. Undergraduates challenged each other to duels, and fought them, despite the best efforts of the faculty to prevent them. They quarreled with and sometimes assaulted merchants in Charlottesville. They threatened and sometimes caned professors, who had to arm themselves to protect their families. Finally, fourteen years after Jefferson died, the situation spiraled completely out of control. When a professor, John Davis, stepped outside his Pavilion (X, Dunglison's old home) to quell a disturbance, he was shot down by a student. Davis had actually been popular with the students, and the murderer was turned in by his fellows—breaking with the code of student *omertá* observed to that point. Two years later the Honor Code was created, which brought into being some of the self-rule that Jefferson had envisaged for his student body.

Jefferson's profound emotional reaction to the early evidence of student violence was connected with the politics of the time. In 1820, three years into his work for the university, the Missouri Compromise was struck by Congress—allowing Missouri to enter the union as a slave state, but restricting slavery henceforth to territory below the latitude 36°30' N. It was this congressional assertion of a power to restrict the sphere of slavery that sent a shudder throughout the South. Jefferson called it "a fire bell in the night." He denied that the federal government had any such right: "To regulate the condition of the different descriptions of men composing a state ... is certainly the exclusive right of every state, which nothing in the Constitution has taken from them and given to the general government." (April 22, 1820) The South, feeling embattled, had hoped to maintain its power by the extra representation given it whenever a slave state was added—the representation of slave residents at a three-fifths ratio. Without that buffer, the region felt vulnerable to assaults on its "peculiar institution." Jefferson put it bluntly:

> For if Congress once goes out of the Constitution to arrogate a right of regulating the condition of the inhabitants of the states, its majority may, and probably will, next declare that the condition of all men within the United States shall be that of freedom; in which case all the whites south of the Potomac and Ohio must evacuate their states, and most fortunate those who can do it first. (Dec. 16, 1820)

Or, as he put it to John Adams, the question was, "are our slaves to be presented with freedom and a dagger." (Jan. 22, 1821)

The southern way of life, which Jefferson praised as morally superior to that of the North, as the protector of "agrarian virtue," was under attack from "restrictionists," who would pen it up, keep it from spreading, and then attack it in its homeland. This gave a new urgency to his work on the university. It must be completed in order to train southern men to defend agrarian virtue. The Missouri action was a direct assault on the South. "The Missouri question is for power." (Jan. 22, 1820) Without a southern university to instill the true agrarian system (with its unfortunate but necessary slave corollary), young men would go north and be poisoned with anti-southern prejudices.

> Harvard will still prime it over us, with her twenty professors. How many of our youths she now has, learning the lessons of anti-Missourianism, I know not; but a gentleman lately from Princeton told he saw the list of the students at that palace, and that more than half were Virginians. These will return home, no doubt, deeply impressed with the sacred principle of our holy alliance of restrictionists. (Jan. 31, 1821)

Those words are taken from the letter in which Jefferson accused Cabell of "desertion" if he did not stay with the effort to save the university even at the risk of his health. The crisis was upon them: "I know well your devotion to your country [Virginia], and your foresight of the awful scenes coming on her, sooner or later. With this foresight, what service can we ever render her equal to this?" As Jefferson wrote to the reactionary John Taylor of Caroline: "These [northern] seminaries are no longer proper for Southern or Western students. The signs of the times admonish us to call them home." (Feb. 14, 1821)

The unnerving spectacle of what southern students were doing at his university raised the question he could not let himself face, the question whether corruption did not come less from cities and banks than from slaveholding. Were these masked ruffians the virtuous yeomen of his ideology? Though he could not bear to face this question, younger members of his family were compelled to face it. His own daughter Martha, seeing a favored slave nanny sold from her husband's bankrupt estate in 1825, wrote to her daughter: "Nothing can prosper under such a system of injustice."[7] That daughter, Jefferson's favorite granddaughter, Ellen, had married a northerner, Joseph Coolidge, the year before; and she wrote back to describe life in New England: "It has given me an idea of prosperity and improvement such as I fear our southern states cannot hope for whilst the canker of slavery eats into their hearts and diseases the whole body by this ulcer at the core."[8] That is just the reaction that Jefferson feared if young Virginians were allowed to go to northern schools.

Apart, even, from such political fears, Jefferson's world seemed to darken around him in the final decade of his life. His debts made it possible that he, like his improvident son-in-law Thomas Mann Randolph, would have to auction off his plantation. Thomas Mann's talented son, named for his grandfather Thomas Jefferson Randolph (and called Jeff), took over much of Jefferson's affairs, though he was only in his twenties. But by the time Jeff reached his thirties, he doubted that those affairs could be salvaged. The $24,000 Jefferson had received from the sale of his library in 1815 had covered only half Jefferson's debt at the time, and heavy borrowing since had put him permanently in arrears of his interest payments. The rector of Central College could not even travel to Rockfish Gap, to gain the site for a new university, without borrowing $100 for expenses of the trip.[9]

To political and financial problems were added family sorrows. His daughter, Martha Randolph, who cared for him and for Monticello, was now in her fifties, overworked and often ill. Her husband, Thomas Mann Randolph, was teetering on the brink of insanity. He had convinced himself that his own son, Jeff, was cheating him out of his estate and that Jefferson had poisoned against him the minds of his wife and children. Robley Dunglison, as the university's professor of medicine, observed these developments with great compassion for Martha and her father in his twice-weekly visits to Monticello. The aberrations of Thomas Mann Randolph, who wanted to hurt Jefferson but was afraid to attack him frontally, came out in a frenetic but feckless campaign he waged in 1825 to defeat Jefferson's great ally, Joseph Cabell, in his campaign for the Senate that year.[10]

Dunglison, like other professors at the university, was invited in rotation to dine at Monticello—just as congressmen had been cycled through dinners at the White House when Jefferson was president. But Dunglison had another reason for being often on the mountain.

> Not long after my arrival at the university Mr. Jefferson found it necessary to consult me in regard to a condition of great instability of the bladder, from which he had suffered for some time, and which inconvenienced him greatly, by the frequent calls to discharge his urine ... On examining the urethra I found that the prostate portion was affected with a stricture, accompanied and apparently produced by an enlargement of the prostate gland ... [which] interfered materially with his horseback exercise on his excellent and gentle horse Eagle, long a favorite with his illustrious master.

Dunglison took a "bougie" (catheter) up the mountain, and taught Jefferson how to insert it himself. But changing symptoms and other ailments made Jefferson depend on regular visits to adjust medication and the dosage of laudanum he was taking for pain. Dunglison had a horse now, and a slave to groom it, for his frequent trips. He became an intimate of the family, always sitting on Jefferson's left side at the dinner table, since Jefferson, increasingly deaf, heard best with that ear.

Some were surprised at Jefferson's reliance on the young doctor, and his deepening respect for him. Dunglison himself wrote: "Mr. Jefferson was considered to have but little faith in physic, and has often told me he would rather trust to the unaided or rather uninterfered-with efforts of nature than to physicians in general." Dunglison probably did not know that Jefferson had once said that doctors were charlatans of the body as theologians were charlatans of the mind. (Sept. 7, 1815) But he knew and laughed at the tale that Jefferson never saw three physicians together without looking for buzzards over their head. Jefferson respected Dunglison because he was a scholar, an empiricist in his practice, and modest about the possibilities of medicine. Later, a famous surgeon who was Dunglison's colleague in Philadelphia, wrote of him: "He despised meddlesome medication and was unsparing in his denunciation of it."[11] Before Dunglison came to America, when he was still in his early twenties, he had published articles in learned journals, so that he received an honorary degree from the Yale school of medicine during his first year in Charlottesville— though the New Haven authorities knew, as yet, so little about the status of education in Virginia that they addressed the honor to Dunglison care of Hampden-Sydney College.

Jefferson trusted Dunglison so thoroughly that he recommended him to Madison as both a friend and a physician. Dunglison also ministered to Martha Randolph, whose efficiency under trying circumstances he admired. He said that he wished she had designed the interior of the university Pavilions—they would have been much more "commodious" in that case. Martha's son Jeff, roughly Dunglison's contemporary, also confided in him, telling him that his mad father had threatened to kill him. After Jefferson's death, when Monticello was deserted and Jeff wanted someone to stay there to keep vandals away, Dunglison moved his family there during the summer break of 1827. (Yes, there was a summer break by then.)

Martha, Jeff, and Dunglison knew what Jefferson tried to hide from himself, the fact that he might be completing his university just as he lost his home. It was nip and tuck whether Jefferson would die under his own roof. One night in his last winter, the seriousness of his plight finally came home to Jefferson, and he devised a desperate scheme to save himself. He would offer all his possessions except his great house as prizes in a lottery to be conducted nationwide. (Economic depression in Virginia made it impossible to sell the land and slaves outright and bring in enough to meet his debts.) Jeff had to break the hard news that even that would not be enough—Monticello, too, would have to be a prize in the lottery, though Jeff was reasonably certain that he could make it a condition that the new owner would take possession only after Jefferson's death. Jefferson composed what would today be called "talking points" for Jeff to show in confidence to Joseph Cabell, who must be recruited to get the legislature's authorization for a lottery.

Cabell ran into strong resistance in the Assembly. Some opposed the lottery on moral grounds, as a form of gambling. Jefferson, too, had opposed gambling in the past but he composed for Jeff's use a casuistical argument that this was not really gambling but a form of reward for public service. Others thought the lottery undignified, and not a matter of state responsibility. If Jefferson wanted recompense for public service, he should petition openly for that. But Cabell, as usual, managed to win authorization in the legislature; and Jeff traveled to New York and New England trying to sell the lottery tickets. He ran into more objections to its gambling aspect, and listened to those who suggested that the tickets just be a form of assistance, all of them to be burnt on the coming Fourth of July, the fiftieth anniversary of the Declaration of Independence. But the Fourth came and there were not enough tickets sold to make a decent fire with. Besides, that was the day Jefferson died.

Dunglison, staying at Monticello to care for his patient, had seen the end coming, as a racking and incessant diarrhea tortured Jefferson. The doctor wrote to Madison tactfully warning him that there was not much time left for seeing Jefferson: "I much fear that, without some speedy amelioration, my worst apprehension must soon be realized." Dunglison watched as his fears came true:

> In the course of the day and night of the second of July, he was affected with stupor, with intervals of wakefulness and consciousness; but on the third, the stupor became permanent. About seven o'clock of the evening of that day, he awoke and seeing my staying at his bedside

exclaimed, "Oh, Doctor, are you still there?"—in a voice, however that was husky and indistinct. He then asked, "Is it the Fourth?"—to which I replied, "It soon will be." These were the last words I heard him utter.

A year before this, the university students had asked for a vacation on the Fourth. In this year, on the fifth of July, they went up the mountain with their teachers, under a threat of rain, to watch as their rector was buried.

EPILOGUE

His University Survives

History swerved impishly into melodrama on the fiftieth anniversary of the signing of the Declaration of Independence. Five hours after Jefferson died on that date, so did John Adams. And before doing so, he said, oracularly but inaccurately: "Thomas Jefferson survives."

Nine years earlier, Adams had guessed, inaccurately, that Jefferson's university would *not* survive:

> I congratulate you and Madison and Monroe on your noble employment in founding a university. From such a noble triumvirate, the world will expect something very great and very new. But if it contains anything quite original, and very excellent, I fear the prejudices are too deeply rooted to suffer it to last long, though it may be accepted at first. It

will not always have three such colossal reputations
to support it.[1]

The university did more than survive; it maintained a continuity with its origins and grew into the great institution it is
today. Even the Civil War was not able to close it down. While
the Rotunda was serving as a military hospital, a reduced corps
of teachers and students held regular sessions throughout.

It was helpful that the "colossal reputations" survived, too,
for quite a time. Madison became rector on Jefferson's death,
and Jefferson's son-in-law Nicholas Trist served as his energetic secretary. Monroe remained on the board until the year
of his death (1831). When Madison resigned in 1834, Joseph
Cabell succeeded him, and Chapman Johnson took over from
Cabell. Several lines of continuity maintained the school's
ties with its founders. James L. Cabell, the nephew of Joseph
Cabell, educated by him as if he were the son he never had,
became the professor of medicine in 1837, and lived in
Pavilion II for fifty-three years. He was a pioneer in develop-
ing preventive medicine and expounding early theories of evo-
lution. Robert Self, descended from another nephew of Joseph
Cabell, owns and lives in the family plantation's great house,
Edgewood, and is now the conservator of architecture and
furniture at Monticello.

Most of the early faculty also served long and honorably.
Those who left did so to fame. Even Key and Long, the misfits
in Virginia, returned to England and became respected members
of the faculty of the University of London, Key as a member
of the Royal Society and Long as a founder of the Royal

Geographical Society. But the most distinguished career awaited Robley Dunglison, who went in 1833 to the hospital in Baltimore, where he had occasion, in Washington, to treat President Andrew Jackson. But his great fame arose at the Jefferson Medical College in Philadelphia, where he became known as "the Father of American Physiology." His medical dictionary was the standard text (he also brought it out in Braille). He was vice president of the American Philosophical Society. A famous surgeon at the Jefferson Medical College was Samuel Gross, whom Thomas Eakins painted in his masterpiece, "The Gross Clinic." Gross said of Dunglison: "Of all the colleagues—nearly forty in number—with whom I have been associated, Robley Dunglison was by far the most learned ... As a profound medical scholar, ages will probably elapse before the profession will have another Dunglison."[2]

At the beginning of the twentieth century, the university finally solved one of its long-standing problems. The board, including Madison, had wanted to create the post of president for the university; but piety toward the expressed view of Jefferson blocked repeated efforts to accomplish this. The first ploy used to circumvent Jefferson's will was the claim that only this position would bring the university a respected law professor (William Wirt). That failed when Wirt refused even the "sweetened" offer. A similar attempt met a similar fate in 1902. Woodrow Wilson, in that year president of Princeton University, had studied at the University of Virginia's law school in 1879-1881 (he lived at No. 31 in the west Range). The board thought it could disarm opposition to a presidency if their famous alumnus could be brought back to his alma mater. But

Wilson, like Wirt, refused the offer. Nonetheless, brisk canvassing of the idea of having a president led to the appointment in 1904 of Edwin A. Alderman (president of Tulane at the time) as the first president of the University of Virginia. He was inaugurated in 1905, and soon took up residence in the grand home, Carr's Hill, designed by Stanford White.

The legacy of Jefferson has built over time a great university, with distinguished and loyal alumni and alumnae (the first women were admitted—to professional and graduate schools—in 1920, though they did not reach the Lawn until the 1970s). The loyalty of the university's graduates is touching, and sometimes deeply sentimental. The architectural curator of Jefferson's buildings at the university, Murray Howard, told me that the Tuscan columns' original color has been recovered—it was a light earth color, not white. Similarly, the dome was not white, but a metallic color like that of its model, the Pantheon. But the white was taken as traditional because of Greek Revival styles, and it is so much a part of the image of the place that its devotees carry in their head that it proves difficult, now, to go back to Jefferson's colors. In fact, when Monticello restored the metal color on its dome, and the earthen hues on the columns of its east portico, Dumas Malone, the great biographer of Jefferson and honored professor of the university, made an emotional plea to William Beiswanger, the curator of Monticello, not to make a case for removing those white features from the Lawn.

Such emotional attachment, along with loyalty of a more substantial sort, has made each generation do its part to justify Jefferson in what he chose to list on his tombstone as his major accomplishments. He did not put there that he was a member of the Continental Congress, governor of Virginia, minister to France, the nation's first secretary of state, its second vice president, its third president. Those things he listed for Jeff Randolph to use in selling lottery tickets to reward his public service. For his tombstone he restricted himself to a more personal list, to the things that mattered most to him, to his identity, to his comfort as he thought of the gains among all his life's losses. He emphatically left instructions that only three achievements be placed on his grave "and not a word more."[3] The first two are short documents he wrote, and it took little more than a day for each to come from his fluent pen. The last took far more time and labor, and it was in constant danger of never being finished at all. When he was persuading Joseph Cabell not to "desert" the effort to create the university, he wrote, "Continue with us in these holy labors until, having seen their accomplishment, we say with old Simeon, *Nunc dimittis, Domine.*" (Jan. 31, 1821) Jefferson even uncharacteristically gave himself a title (father) that was never official—in life he was always and only called rector. This last of his three great feats is in good company on the tomb, and it deserves to be.

HERE WAS BURIED
THOMAS JEFFERSON
AUTHOR OF THE DECLARATION
OF AMERICAN INDEPENDENCE
OF THE STATUTE OF VIRGINIA
FOR RELIGIOUS FREEDOM
AND FATHER OF THE UNIVERSITY OF VIRGINIA

APPENDIX 1

First Inhabitants of the Pavilions

PAVILION I: John Patton Emmet, Natural History (chemistry, geology, mineralogy, zoology, and botany)

PAVILION II: Thomas Johnson, Demonstrator (not Professor) of Anatomy and Surgery, subordinate to the Professor of Medicine

PAVILION III: John Tayloe Lomax, Law (comprising government, political economy, and law of nations)

PAVILION IV: George Blaettermann, Modern Languages

PAVILION V: George Long, Ancient Languages

PAVILION VI: Charles Bonnycastle, Natural Philosophy (comprising logic and scientific principles)

PAVILION VII: At first a library and meeting room, then a chapel from 1832 to 1855, now the Colonnade Club

PAVILION VIII: Thomas Key, Mathematics

PAVILION IX: George Tucker, Moral Philosophy (comprising ethics and aesthetics)

PAVILION X: Robley Dunglison, Medicine

APPENDIX 2

University of Virginia Chronology

I. PREHISTORY

1729-1731: George Berkeley, in Newport, R. I., works on project for College of Bermuda.

1771: Jefferson draws plan for addition to Wren Building at William and Mary.

1779: Committee for the Revision of the Laws of Virginia submits to the legislature Jefferson's three-tier "Bill for the More General Diffusion of Knowledge."

1780: As governor of Virginia, Jefferson proposes reforms for the college of William and Mary.

1795: Jefferson asks George Washington to transfer the College of Geneva to Virginia.

1799: As VP, Jefferson judges American Philosophical Society's competition for national university plan (Samuel Knox wins with a design of concentric squares).

1800:	Pierre-Samuel du Pont de Nemours publishes plan for national university in United States.
1804:	L. W. Tazewell, in the House of Delegates, asks Jefferson to draw up a proposal for a state university.
1805:	Virginia governor John Taylor asks Jefferson for views on state education.
1809-1810:	Virginia legislature establishes Literary Fund for schools.
1810:	Jefferson responds to trustees' request for a proposed Tennessee university with a plan for "an academical village."
1813:	Joseph Jacques Ramée creates a plan for Union College.

II. CREATING THE UNIVERSITY

1814:	Jefferson named to the board of Albemarle Academy (chartered in 1804 but never opened). The board petitions the Assembly to become Central College.
1815:	Peter Carr, Jefferson's nephew, does not submit the Central College petition because of ill health. Assembly distracted by War of 1812.
1816:	Joseph Cabell champions petition for Central College, which is granted, though no funds are voted for it. Governor appoints six-man board for the college, which includes Jefferson. He is elected rector by his fellow board members.
1817:	Board of Central College chooses its site, near Charlottesville. Jefferson asks for ideas on its buildings from William Thornton and Benjamin Latrobe. Begins first building (which will become Pavilion

VII). Board of Central College petitions Assembly for permission to become the University of Virginia.

1818: Legislature appoints commission to choose a site for the university. The commission meets at Rockfish Gap, and chooses Charlottesville for the site. Work is begun on Pavilions III and V.

1819: Legislature brings the University of Virginia into existence. Arthur Brockenbrough appointed proctor in charge of construction. Jefferson designs the East Pavilions.

1820: Seven Pavilions under construction.

1821: The Neilson plan is drawn.

1822: Maverick's engraving made from Neilson plan. Hotels finished. Rotunda begun.

1823: Funds for Rotunda approved by legislature.

1824: Francis Walker Gilmer sent to Europe for professors, hires five. Lafayette visits university and attends banquet in Rotunda. First two professors arrive, from England.

1825: Five professors arrive, three from England. Classes begin. Jefferson designs Anatomical Theater. First student riots. Board of Visitors impose new rules of discipline.

1826: Thomas Jefferson dies July 4.

1826-1834: James Madison serves as second rector.

1827: Anatomical Theater finished.

III. SUBSEQUENT HISTORY

1832: Chapel held in Pavilion VII.

1837-1890: Dr. James L. Cabell, nephew of Joseph Cabell, teaches medicine from Pavilion II

1840:   Murder of Professor John Davis.

1842:   Honor Code adopted.

1845-1873: William McGuffy succeeds George Tucker as professor of moral philosophy, writes his famous *Readers* in
Pavilion IX, helps found first University YMCA (in
1858), and helps keep the university functioning
during the Civil War.

1851-1853: Robert Mills builds Annex to Rotunda.

1856-1875: Basil Gildersleeve, America's greatest classical scholar, teaches Greek from Pavilion I, taking time off in
campaign seasons to fight in the Confederate
Army—and is wounded in 1864 as a courier for
General John B. Gordon.

1879-1881: Woodrow Wilson a student in the law school.

1895:   Fire at Rotunda.

1896-1898: Stanford White restores Rotunda, closes Lawn at
south with three buildings (Cabell Hall, Cocke Hall,
Rouss Hall).

1902:   Woodrow Wilson is offered the presidency of the
university.

1905:   First president of the university installed (Edwin A.
Alderman).

1907-1909: President's residence, Carr's Hill, built to Stanford
White's design.

1920:   Women students first admitted to the university (in
graduate and professional schools).

1923-1926: Extensive repairs made to Rotunda.

1924:   Basil Gildersleeve buried in university cemetery.

1950:	Gregory H. Swanson becomes the first black student admitted (in the law school).
1951:	Robert F. Kennedy graduates from law school.
1959:	Edward M. Kennedy graduates from law school.
1973-1976:	Rotunda interior returned to Jefferson's configuration.

Notes

PROLOGUE   *Jefferson as Artist*

[1]Ruskin was describing the west cathedral front at Pisa, in *The Seven Lamps of Architecture,* Chapter 5, "The Lamp of Life" (George Allen, 1905), Vol. 8, p. 204.

CHAPTER 2   *New World Artifact*

[1] Paul Venable Turner, *Campus: An American Planning Tradition* (MIT Press, 1984), p. 6.

[2] In 1918, the Gothic exponent, Ralph Adams Cram, attacked the early college architecture of America as "puritan" when it was not following the "pompous [classical] style President Jefferson did so much to advance." Ibid., p. 217.

[3] Most early Catholic colleges were an exception to the antiurban policy, since Catholics were happy to stress their European connections and to be near the seat of a bishop or to a major urban church.

[4] William B. O'Neal, *Jefferson's Buildings at the University of Virginia: The Rotunda* (University of Virginia Press, 1960), p. 42.

[5] Ibid., p. 53.

CHAPTER 3   *Dialogue with Nature*

[1] Franco Barbieri, *Architetture palladiane: Dall pratica del cantiere alle immagini del Trattato* (Neri Pozza Editore, 1992), pp. 58-59.

[2] Ibid., pp. 135-44, 199-208.

[3] Lewis Mumford, *The South in Architecture* (Harcourt, Brace and Company, 1941), pp. 70-71: "The scale and character of the building—the Rotunda—are entirely out of keeping with the village plan that Jefferson wisely had in mind ... [nor] is it anything but an awkward overgrown structure, which mars the general picture ..."

CHAPTER 4   *Latrobe*

[1] Joseph Lasala, "Jefferson's Designs for the University of Virginia" M. A. Thesis, University of Virginia, 1992, p. 17-04.

[2] Philip Alexander Bruce, *History of the University of Virginia, 1819-1919* (Macmillan, 1920). Vol. 1, p. 187. The work's five volumes cover only the first hundred years of the institution, and certain archaic attitudes must be allowed for—e.g., the treatment of women, or of the "paladins and martyrs"of

the Confederacy. But the volumes are a great storehouse of information.

3 Lasala, op. cit., p. 17.

4 On the other hand, preservationist purity lost a recent battle—over restoring Madison's plantation great house at Montpelier. This involves removing the additions the Duponts made to the home during the long period when they owned it. Its "restoration" must be more conjectural than that of the Rotunda, since Montpelier lacks the written and drawn record of the construction that Rotunda restorers used in the 1970s. There are photographs of the dome room, unaltered since Jefferson's day, taken before the fire in 1895, for which there are no equivalents at Montpelier. There *is* an authentic core of Madisonian structure under the Dupontisms, and the additions to that core were gradual and inartistic, with no Stanford White to impose a single concept on them, which makes them little worth preserving.

CHAPTER 5 *"Universal Confessors" Arrive*

1 All the following quotes from Dunglison are from his manuscript diary, "Autobiographical Ana," which is in the library of the College of Physicians of Philadelphia. It is a lively account, important to the history of medicine in America, one that should be edited for publication. I quote from the parts of the diary dealing with Dunglison's time at the University of Virginia, which I read on microfilm in the Alderman Library.

2 Dumas Malone, *The Sage of Monticello* (Little, Brown and Company, 1981), p. 399.

³ Richard Beale Davis, *Francis Walker Gilmer* (The Dietz Press, 1939), p. 201.

⁴ Ibid., p. 134.

⁵ Ibid., p. 228.

⁶ Malone, op. cit., p. 465.

⁷ Ibid., p. 460.

⁸ Ibid., p. 461.

⁹ Ibid., p. 304.

¹⁰ Ibid., p. 454.

¹¹ The words are those of Samuel Gross, in John M. Dorsey, M.D., *The Jefferson-Dunglison Letters* (University of Virginia Press, 1960), p. 87.

EPILOGUE   *His University Survives*

¹ Adams to Jefferson, May 26, 1817, in Lester J. Cappon (ed.), *The Adams-Jefferson Letters* (University of North Carolina Press, 1959), Vol. 2, p. 518.

² John M. Dorsey, M.D., *The Jefferson-Dunglison Letters* (University of Virginia Press, 1960), pp. 86-87.

³ Merrill D. Peterson, *Thomas Jefferson: Writings* (The Library of America, 1984), p. 706.

Illustrations Credits

FRONTISPIECE. Plan of the University [of Virginia], Peter Maverick, engraver, January-February 1822. Courtesy of The Papers of Thomas Jefferson, Albert and Shirley Small Special Collections Library, University of Virginia Library, adapted from the original

FIGURE 1. Panoramic view of the Rotunda and the Lawn, University of Virginia, from the south, 1909. Mss. 9978, 4x5-749. Courtesy of the Rector and Visitors of the University of Virginia

FIGURE 2. Arcade on West Range, University of Virginia. Courtesy of Bill Sublette, University of Virginia

FIGURE 3. Path from Range toward Lawn, past serpentine walls, University of Virginia. Courtesy of Garry Wills

FIGURE 4. Pavilion VII, University of Virginia. Courtesy of Bill Sublette, University of Virginia

FIGURE 5. Pavilion VIII, University of Virginia. Courtesy of Bill Sublette, University of Virginia

FIGURE 6. Pavilion V, University of Virginia. Courtesy of Bill Sublette, University of Virginia

FIGURE 7. Pavilion IX, University of Virginia. Courtesy of Bill Sublette, University of Virginia

FIGURE 8. Pavilion X, University of Virginia. Courtesy of Bill Sublette, University of Virginia

FIGURE 9. Joseph Jacques Ramée, plan for Union College, ca 1812. Courtesy of Schaffer Library, Special Collections, Union College, Schenectady, New York

FIGURE 10. Benjamin Henry Latrobe, first floor plan of a Military Academy, January 26, 1800. Courtesy of Benjamin Henry Latrobe Archive, The Library of Congress

FIGURE 11. Pavilion III, University of Virginia. Courtesy of Bill Sublette, University of Virginia

FIGURE 12. Thomas Jefferson, study of the first and second floor plans of the Anatomical Theater, east elevation and section, University of Virginia, 1825. Courtesy of The Papers of

Thomas Jefferson, Albert and Shirley Small Special Collections Library, University of Virginia Library

FIGURE 13. Monticello, north pavilion and west portico. Courtesy of Garry Wills

FIGURE 14. Rotunda, University of Virginia. Courtesy of Bill Sublette, University of Virginia

FIGURE 15. Thomas Jefferson, 1748-1826. N056/K031. Monticello, dependencies (plan) before August 4, 1772. MHS Image number 1476. Courtesy of The Massachusetts Historical Society

FIGURE 16. Benjamin Henry Latrobe (?), west facade of Pavilion X, University of Virginia, N-353, K Pl. 17, L-10-03. Courtesy of The Papers of Thomas Jefferson, Albert and Shirley Small Special Collections Library, University of Virginia Library

FIGURE 17. Benjamin Henry Latrobe (?), view of the Rotunda with Pavilions IX and X, February 1823. N-354. Courtesy of The Papers of Thomas Jefferson, Albert and Shirley Small Special Collections Library, University of Virginia Library

FIGURE 18. Plan for the ground floor of the Désert de Retz, built by Racine de Monville, ca 1785. Courtesy of The Royal Library, National Library of Sweden

FIGURE 19. Thomas Jefferson, plan for the first floor of the

Rotunda, University of Virginia, July 16, 1823. N-330, K-10, L-17-02. Courtesy of The Papers of Thomas Jefferson, Albert and Shirley Small Special Collections Library, University of Virginia Library

FIGURE 20. Rotunda interior staircase, after restoration, University of Virginia, 1976. RG-5/7/2.821, Negative # PS740140.58. Courtesy of Manuscripts Print Collection, Albert and Shirley Small Special Collections Library, University of Virginia Library

FIGURE 21. Rotunda dome room, after restoration, University of Virginia, 1976. RG-5/7/2.821, Negative # PS760124. Courtesy of Manuscripts Print Collection, Albert and Shirley Small Special Collections Library, University of Virginia Library

FIGURE 22. Rotunda interior, University of Virginia, A. L. Hench, ca 1940. Prints # 130, Negative # 4x5-1046-E. Courtesy of Manuscripts Print Collection, Albert and Shirley Small Special Collections Library, University of Virginia Library

Acknowledgments

My first debt is to Murray Howard, the curator for historic buildings at the University of Virginia. A practicing architect, he was finishing his twenty years of service to the university when I met him. He spent several days showing me around the buildings, discussing their construction, maintenance, and restoration. He taught restoration by engaging the students in his work on the structures, so his explanations were pedagogically effective. He also found me lodging on the Lawn, through his membership in the Colonnade Club, in a front room of the first building raised by Jefferson (Pavilion VII).

My next debt is to Malcolm Bell, of the art history department at the university. His exciting new hypotheses about Latrobe's role in the university's design are a work in progress, to be published by the University of Virginia. He generously shared some of his explorations with me, by interview and correspondence. I remember especially a long interview, on an improbably warm February day, conducted on the balcony of Pavilion VII. By one account, Jefferson's last visit to the Lawn was to inspect the library volumes being stored in this Pavilion, after which he sat on the balcony and watched an imported Corinthian capital being attached to the first column raised on the Rotunda portico. Trees now intercept that view; but it was a very appropriate place for me to learn more about Latrobe and the Lawn.

Frank Grizzard, now an associate editor of the George Washington papers being published by the university, steered me to important Jeffersonian sources, none more so than his own essential chronology of the funding and construction of the original buildings. Michael Plunkett, director of special collections at the Alderman Library, introduced me to the riches in the university's online collection of historic papers and photographs.

On things Jeffersonian in general I am always learning from that man so deeply acquainted with him, Douglas Wilson, until recently the director of the Jeffersonian International Center at Kenwood.

My friends at Monticello were helpful, as always—Daniel Jordan, Susan Stein, and Lucia Stanton. Robert Self, the conservator of architecture and furniture at Monticello, showed me through his workshop and conducted me around the house to show what kinds of work he is called on to perform in maintaining and restoring Jefferson's original fabric.

My master agent is Andrew Wylie. On this book, his assistants Zoë Pagnamenta and Anne Jump were continually helpful.

I thank Feldman and Associates for the photo research.

ABOUT THE AUTHOR

Garry Wills is an adjunct professor of history at Northwestern University. He is the author of many books, including *Lincoln at Gettysburg, Papal Sin, Venice: Lion City, Saint Augustine, James Madison,* and *What Jesus Meant.* He has been awarded the Pulitzer Prize, the Presidential Medal of the National Endowment for the Humanities, and the National Book Critics Circle Award.

This book is set in Garamond 3, designed by
Morris Fuller Benton and Thomas Maitland
Cleland in the 1930s, and Monotype Grotesque,
both released digitally by Adobe.

Printed by R. R. Donnelley and Sons on
Gladfelter 60-pound Thor Offset smooth
white antique paper.

Cover printed by Moore Langen Printing.
Color separation by Quad Graphics.